The Growth and Influence of Islam
IN THE NATIONS OF ASIA AND CENTRAL ASIA

Muslims in China

The Growth and Influence of Islam

IN THE NATIONS OF ASIA AND CENTRAL ASIA

Afghanistan

Azerbaijan

Bangladesh

Indonesia

Islam in Asia: Facts and Figures

Islamism and Terrorist Groups in Asia

Kazakhstan

The Kurds

Kyrgyzstan

Malaysia

Muslims in China

Muslims in India

Muslims in Russia

Pakistan

Tajikistan

Turkmenistan

Uzbekistan

The Growth and Influence of Islam
IN THE NATIONS OF ASIA AND CENTRAL ASIA

Muslims in China

Sheila Hollihan-Elliot

Mason Crest Publishers
Philadelphia

Produced by OTTN Publishing, Stockton, New Jersey

Mason Crest Publishers
370 Reed Road
Broomall, PA 19008
www.masoncrest.com

First printing

1 3 5 7 9 8 6 4 2

Library of Congress Cataloging-in-Publication Data

Applied for
ISBN 1-59084-880-2

Table of Contents

Chinese Uyghurs participate in mid-afternoon prayers at a mosque in Turpan.

Dr. Harvey Sicherman, president and director of the Foreign Policy Research Institute, is the author of such books as *America the Vulnerable: Our Military Problems and How to Fix Them* (2002) and *Palestinian Autonomy, Self-Government and Peace* (1993).

Introduction

by Dr. Harvey Sicherman

America's triumph in the Cold War promised a new burst of peace and prosperity. Indeed, the decade between the demise of the Soviet Union and the destruction of September 11, 2001, proved deceptively hopeful. Today, of course, we are more fully aware—to our sorrow—of the dangers and troubles no longer just below the surface.

The Muslim identities of most of the terrorists at war with the United States have also provoked great interest in Islam as well as the role of religion in politics. It is crucial for Americans not to assume that Osama bin Laden's ideas are identical to those of most Muslims or, for that matter, that most Muslims are Arabs. A truly world religion, Islam claims hundreds of millions of adherents, from every ethnic group scattered across the globe. This book series covers the growth and influence of Muslims in Asia and Central Asia.

A glance at the map establishes the extraordinary coverage of our authors. Every climate and terrain may be found, along with every form of human society, from the nomadic groups of the Central Asian steppes to

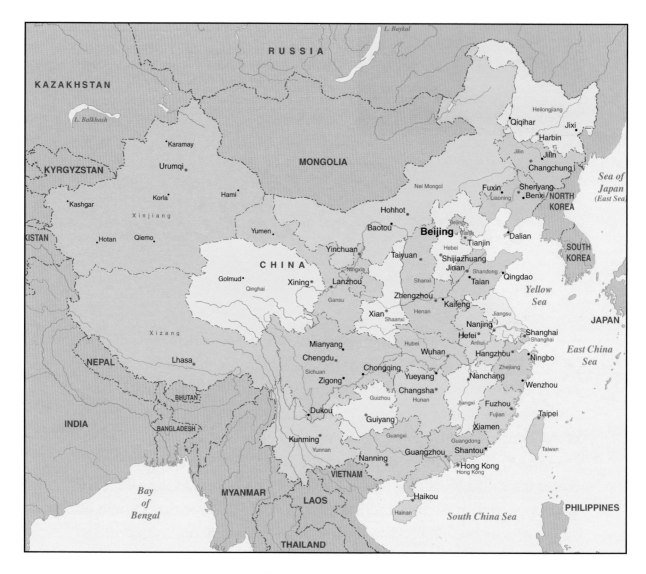

highly sophisticated cities such as Singapore, New Delhi, and Shanghai. The economies of the nations examined in this series are likewise highly diverse. In some, barter systems are still used; others incorporate modern stock markets. In some of the countries, large oil reserves hold out the prospect of prosperity. Other countries, such as India and China, have progressed by moving from a government-controlled to a more market-based economic system. Still other countries have built wealth on service and shipping.

Central Asia and Asia is a heavily armed and turbulent area. Three of its states (China, India, and Pakistan) are nuclear powers, and one (Kazakhstan) only recently rid itself of nuclear weapons. But it is also a place where the horse and mule remain indispensable instruments of war. All of the region's states have an extensive history of conflict, domestic and international, old and new. Afghanistan, for example, has known little but invasion and civil war over the past two decades.

Governments include dictatorships, democracies, and hybrids without a name; centralized and decentralized administrations; and older patterns of tribal and clan associations. The region is a veritable encyclopedia of political expression.

Although such variety defies easy generalities, it is still possible to make several observations. First, the geopolitics of Central Asia and Asia reflect the impact of empires and the struggles of post-imperial independence. Central Asia, a historic corridor for traders and soldiers, was the scene of Russian expansion well into Soviet times. While Kazakhstan's leaders participated in the historic meeting of December 25, 1991, that dissolved the Soviet Union, the rest of the region's newly independent republics hardly expected it. They have found it difficult to grapple with a sometimes tenuous independence, buffeted by a strong residual Russian influence, the absence of settled institutions, the temptation of newly valuable natural resources, and mixed populations lacking a solid national identity. The shards of the Soviet Union have often been sharp—witness the Russian war in Chechnya—and sometimes fatal for those ambitious to grasp them.

Moving further east, one encounters an older devolution, that of the half-century since the British Raj dissolved into India and Pakistan (the latter giving violent birth to Bangladesh in 1971). Only recently, partly under the impact of the war on terrorism, have these nuclear-armed neighbors and adversaries found it possible to renew attempts at reconciliation. Still further east, Malaysia shares a British experience, but Indonesia has been influenced by its Dutch heritage. Even China defines its own borders along the lines of the Qing empire (the last pre-republican dynasty) at its most expansionist (including Tibet and Taiwan). These imperial histories lie heavily upon the politics of the region.

A second aspect worth noting is the variety of economic experimentation afoot in the area. State-dominated economic strategies, still in the ascendant, are separating government from the actual running of commerce and industry. "Privatization," however, is frequently a byword for crony capitalism and corruption. Yet in dynamic economies such as that of China, as well as an increasingly productive India, hundreds of millions of people have dramatically improved both their standard of living and their hope for the future. All of them aspire to benefit from international trade. Competitive advantages, such as low-cost labor (in some cases trained in high technology) and valuable natural resources (oil, gas, and minerals), promise much. This is indeed a revolution of rising expectations, some of which are being satisfied.

Yet more than corruption threatens this progress. Population increase, even though moderating, still overwhelms educational and employment opportunities. Many countries are marked by extremes of wealth and poverty, especially between rural and urban areas. Dangerous jealousies threaten ethnic groups (such as anti-Chinese violence in Indonesia). Hopelessly overburdened public services portend turmoil. Public health, never adequate, is harmed further by environmental damage to critical resources (such as the Aral Sea). By and large, Central Asian and Asian countries are living well beyond their infrastructures.

Third and finally, Islam has deeply affected the states and peoples of the region. Indonesia is the largest Muslim state in the world, and India hosts the second-largest Muslim population. Islam is not only the official religion of many states, it is the very reason for Pakistan's existence. But Islamic practices and groups vary: the well-known Sunni and Shiite groups are joined by energetic Salafi (Wahabi) and Sufi movements. Over the last 20 years especially, South and Central Asia have become battlegrounds for competing Shiite (Iranian) and Wahabi (Saudi) doctrines, well financed from abroad and aggressively antagonistic toward non-Muslims and each other. Resistance to the Soviet invasion of Afghanistan brought these groups battle-tested warriors and organizers. The war on terrorism has exposed just how far-reaching and active the new advocates of holy war (jihad) can be. Indonesia, in particular, is the scene of rivalry between an older, tolerant Islam and the jihadists. But Pakistan also faces an Islamic identity crisis. And India, wracked by sectarian strife, must hold together its democratic framework despite Muslim and Hindu extremists. This newly significant struggle within Islam, superimposed on an older Muslim history, will shape political and economic destinies throughout the region and beyond. Hence, the focus of our series.

We hope that these books will enlighten both teacher and student about a critical subject in a critical area of the world. Central Asia and Asia would be important in their own right to Americans; arguably, after 9/11, they became vital to our national security. And the enduring impact of Islam is a crucial factor we must understand. We at the Foreign Policy Research Institute hope these books will illuminate both the facts and the prospects.

The signs at the entrance to this mosque are written in both Arabic and Chinese. Although Muslims make up only a small percentage of China's population, the Muslim community in China is believed to be about 20 million.

Overview

The origins of Chinese civilization have been traced back to Neolithic times (around 10,000 B.C.), when small farming communities were established in the river valleys of the vast China plain. Today, the Chinese proudly note that theirs is the longest continuously existing civilization. Over time, however, the unique Chinese civilization has been refreshed and invigorated by exposure to outside influences. *Islam*, which arrived in China after the seventh century A.D., was one of those outside influences.

Although historically China has included members of many different *ethnic groups*, its culture has been cohesive because of shared values. The Chinese reverence for history contributed to the development of writing, and Chinese culture stressed education as the primary way for the ambitious to advance in society.

13

While the Chinese developed many new inventions, such as the compass, clock, and fireworks, they also showed a knack for learning about something new, copying and adapting it to Chinese needs, and often re-exporting the now improved innovation for lucrative trade. China's long history of civilization is displayed through the architecture, monuments, writings, and decorative arts that interest modern tourists and China scholars.

The Chinese are justifiably proud of their advanced civilization, and throughout history they have tended to look with disdain upon non-Chinese, considering them crude barbarians. This attitude has proven problematic for **Muslims** in China, particularly in the past two centuries.

China's Traditional World View

Loyalty and respect feature strongly in Chinese culture. The Chinese believe that the dead continue to live in a spirit world parallel to the physical world, and that dead ancestors continue to influence events here on earth. Thus, family members who are still living must give respect and gifts to the dead. The term "ancestor worship" is often used in the West to describe this practice, but it is more accurate to define it as continuing to care for ancestors in the spirit world, rather than worship.

Four thousand years ago, a tribe that succeeded in uniting and ruling much of China, the Xia, believed the ancient founder of their **dynasty** continued to rule through his descendants. This is why the emperors were called "Son of Heaven." Over millennia, this concept evolved into the idea of a remote God in the Heavens who could take away the "mandate to rule" from one family and award it to a deserving family that succeeded in seizing the power to rule. This belief system enabled the Chinese to justify changes in imperial dynasties. As each ruling dynasty became corrupt, it was overthrown, often through a peasant-supported rebellion.

At about the same time the Xia dynasty ruled China, a new religious idea—monotheism, or the belief in one God—was emerging in the Middle

East. Around the year 2000 B.C., a man named Abraham committed himself to follow and obey one God—a radical concept in a time when all other religions featured numerous deities, many of which had to be regularly appeased through prayer or sacrifice. Abraham's faith became the basis for Judaism. Two monotheistic religions related to Judaism, Christianity and Islam, would later emerge. Both Christians and Muslims claim Abraham as a spiritual ancestor and say they believe in the same God as Jews. Through the efforts of Christian and Muslim missionaries monotheism would become the dominant religious form in the world.

The Temple of Heaven in Beijing was built as a place for the Ming emperors to offer sacrifices. The worldview of ancient China, which developed over thousands of years, was far different from the world view of the Muslims who arrived after the seventh century A.D.

This Persian miniature painting shows the Patriarch Abraham being visited by an angel. Abraham is sometimes called the first monotheist, and is considered the spiritual father of Judaism, Christianity, and Islam.

In all three of these monotheistic religions, God is seen as the universal lawgiver, providing a set of rules by which all men are expected to live. According to Christian and Muslim theology, after death those who obeyed God's commandments and lived a good life will be rewarded in Heaven. Those who did not will be punished in Hell.

Monotheism never gained the widespread appeal in China that it did in Europe and Central Asia. Instead, over centuries the Chinese developed a varied religion, based on assorted spirit gods. The Chinese also embraced Buddhism during the rule of the Tang dynasty (A.D. 618–907). Where monotheists believe God has constructed a framework of laws that humans must obey, the Chinese turned to teachers like Confucius to explain how human society should function. Confucius (551–479 B.C.) lived in a period during which China was torn by internal wars. During his life he encouraged reforms that would bring peace. In his book *A Short History of China and Southeast Asia: Tribute, Trade, and Influence*, author Martin Stuart-Fox writes:

> Confucius had one overriding concern: to restore social order and moral propriety in an age of growing political anarchy and social chaos. . . . It was essential that everyone should know their place in the world, accept their duties and responsibilities, and recognize their superiors and inferiors. Moral example should be provided by those at the apex of the hierarchy, and emulated by their inferiors. . . . The moral qualities Confucius prized included first and foremost *ren*, sometimes translated as "humanheartedness" or "humaneness," meaning something like philanthropic benevolence towards others and concerns for their well-being.

Confucianism remained the basis for China's culture and society until the 20th century.

The Development of Islam

The word *Islam* comes from an Arabic verb meaning "to surrender" or "to submit." Muslims, or followers of Islam, believe that they are submitting to the will of the one God, whom they call **Allah**. The most important human figure is a man named Muhammad, who established the religion after receiving a series of messages from Allah in the seventh century A.D.

The polytheistic Arab society of the Arabian Peninsula, where Muhammad lived, was nomadic, violent, and cruel. Muhammad was a pious and respected merchant, and each year he spent time alone in a cave outside the city of Mecca, where he prayed and meditated. According to Muslim tradition, when Muhammad was about 40 years old he was sleeping in the cave when an angel appeared. The angel told Muhammad that he was to reveal to the world that there was only one God.

Eventually, Muhammad began to teach others Allah's messages, and he gradually gained a small group of followers. However, his message angered the wealthy and powerful people of Mecca, and they began to persecute Muhammad and his followers. In A.D. 622, the small group of Muslims left Mecca secretly and moved to another city, Yathrib. In the Arab culture of the time, their leaving was considered a betrayal, and the Meccans vowed to destroy the Muslims. However, the Muslim community flourished in Yathrib and fought off several attacks by the Meccans. By 630, Muhammad and his followers were strong enough to capture Mecca, after which most of the city's residents converted to Islam. By the time of Muhammad's death in 632 many of the Arab tribes had been united under Islam.

The teachings of Muhammad became the basis for the new religion. After Muhammad's death, his saying were collected and compiled into a book called the **Qur'an**. Muslims believe this holy scripture is the word of Allah, and try to live according to its teachings. Stories about Muhammad and other devout early Muslims, known as the **Hadith**, provide examples for how people ought to behave.

The religion has five major precepts, known as the Five Pillars of Islam. The first is a profession of faith, in which the Muslim declares, "There is no god but Allah, and Muhammad is His messenger." The second is the requirement that Muslims must perform five prayers at certain times during each day. Third is the duty to give to charity and help the poor. The fourth pillar is the obligation to abstain from eating, drinking, and other activities during Ramadan, the ninth month of the Islamic lunar calendar. Ramadan is considered a holy month, and while fasting Muslims are expected to focus on Allah. The fifth pillar is the requirement that all Muslims make a pilgrimage to Mecca, the holy city, at least once during their lifetimes if they are physically and financially able to do so.

Some of the teachings and stories of Islam come from two earlier monotheistic religions, Judaism and Christianity. Muslims believe that the major figures of those religions—such as Abraham, Moses, and Jesus—were prophets to whom God revealed His true religion. But over time, their followers made mistakes passing the information from one generation to another, corrupting God's message to humanity. Muslims believe Islam is the final revelation of the truth, and corrects the errors that had crept into Judaism and Christianity. This belief gives Muslims a strong desire to spread their religion so that all people can join the brotherhood of those submitting to Allah.

Muhammad's teachings made the new religion attractive to many people, and Islam soon spread far beyond the Arabian Peninsula. One hundred years after Muhammad's death, under political and religious leaders known as caliphs, the Muslims had conquered an empire that stretched from the Iberian Peninsula (modern-day Spain and Portugal) and North Africa to the Middle East, Persia, and Eastern Europe. The religion spread east into Africa and Asia during the eighth and ninth centuries, but in general it was brought by traders and missionaries rather than by conquering armies.

Chinese and Muslim Cultures

It was inevitable that China, with its ancient civilization, would eventually come into contact with this vital new religious force. Speaking

A devout Muslim prays in the Great Mosque at Mecca; in the center is a square black building called the Kaaba, which is considered the holiest place in Islam. Muslims are expected to make a pilgrimage to Mecca at least once during their lifetimes.

generally, there were many similarities between the value systems of Chinese and Muslims in the eighth and ninth centuries. Like the Chinese, the Muslims respected learning, and their schools and universities were famous for their open discourse and pursuit of knowledge. Calligraphy is considered one of the four "treasures" of Chinese art, and because of Islamic restrictions against creating images of living things calligraphy became an important Muslim art form as well. Both the Chinese and Muslims followed religious rituals, as well as specific rules on the treatment of women and slaves.

There were, of course, many differences as well. Muslims believe that there will be a Day of Judgment, on which the faithful will be admitted to Heaven, while the Chinese do not believe in the idea of an ultimate judgment. Because Muslims believe submission to Allah and adherence to the teachings of Muhammad are required for salvation, they actively try to convert others. The Chinese, on the other hand, have traditionally taken a more tolerant and inclusive view of religion. In Chinese thought, an individual could follow Taoism, recite Buddhist prayers, or beseech folk gods or benevolent ancestors, depending on his or her need at a particular moment. Islam also taught that all Muslims are equal in the eyes of Allah, while Chinese society had a highly structured class system.

Perhaps the major difference between the two civilizations is the matter of allegiance. The Chinese system teaches that the emperor is the ultimate authority on earth, while Islam teaches that, through the caliphs, Allah is the final authority. As Martin Stuart-Fox explains in *A Short History of China and Southeast Asia*:

> Acceptance of Islam drew a region into an alternative international order, one that looked to sultan or caliph as primus inter pares among Muslim rulers, designated by Allah to preside over the congregation of believers. Such a worldview allowed no cosmic dimension for the Son of Heaven. . . . Chinese power might be respected, to the point where rulers of minor Muslim states were prepared to do the kowtow before Chinese emperors, but the cosmic basis of the Chinese world order could never be accommodated by Islam.

At times, this critical difference has proven to be problematic in the history of Muslims in China.

Today, the Chinese government officially recognizes 56 different minority groups living within China. Among them are several groups that predominantly practice Islam. Although exact figures are not available, according to data from China's 2000 census between 1 and 2 percent of

A Uyghur man (left) speaks with a Han Chinese man on a street in Ürümqi. The Han are the dominant Chinese ethnic group, representing about 92 percent of China's population. Uyghurs are one of several ethnic minorities in China that predominantly practice Islam.

Chinese are Muslims. That would be a small number in many countries, but because China has the world's largest population (more than 1.2 billion people), it means the Muslim population of China is around 20 million.

According to the official doctrine of the ruling Communist Party, all groups within China are equal and get along together. In reality, however, there remains an underlying antipathy between some **Han** Chinese (the dominant group in China) and Chinese Muslims. Han Chinese traditionally consider themselves the "real" Chinese, with a superior culture, and see Muslims as outsiders. In turn, some Muslims are contemptuous of the Han, who they view as corrupt and irreligious. Despite the efforts of the government, long-standing attitudes are impossible to legislate away.

And although in general the government tries to maintain good relations with China's Muslim citizens, it is also trying to stamp out a **separatist** movement among Muslims in western China. Some **Uyghurs**, who live in the Xinjiang province of western China, are attempting to break away from China and create an independent country. The government has used harsh methods to repress this movement, and has promised never to allow independence for the Uyghurs.

Workers excavate a Buddhist statue dating from the Tang Dynasty in Xi'an. It was during Tang rule, from 618 to 907, that Muslims first arrived in China. According to a Hadith, or story about Muhammad, the Muslim leader encouraged his followers, "Seek knowledge even if it is in China."

2

Islam Comes to the Middle Kingdom

In A.D. 622 the Prophet Muhammad established the first community governed by Islamic principles in Yathrib, a small oasis settlement on the Arabian Peninsula. From this minor city, the Arab Muslims expanded their authority far beyond the Arabian Peninsula. By the early tenth century the Arab Muslim caliphs ruled a vast empire that included most of the Middle East, North Africa, the Iberian Peninsula of Western Europe, and Central Asia.

At roughly the same time, a new ruling dynasty, the Tang, held power in China. The Tang dynasty, which lasted from 618 to 907, brilliantly revived China's imperial splendor. Like other vigorous new dynasties in China's history, once Tang power was assured the emperors sought to expand their hegemony far beyond the borders they had inherited. As the Muslims expanded east and the Chinese west, it was inevitable that eventually their two worlds would meet.

Reasons for Chinese Expansion

The reasons for the Tang dynasty's expansion were based in the Chinese view of the world. The Chinese believed that the entire world (or, "all under Heaven") was made up of five concentric and interrelated zones. At the center was the area under direct control of the Tang emperor. Immediately outside of this was the region controlled by powerful feudal lords, who were loyal to the emperor. Next came areas where the people adhered to Chinese culture, but were not part of the empire. This was known as the pacified zone. Collectively, these three regions were known as the Middle Kingdom. Outside them were two zones where non-Chinese lived: an inner zone for those who accepted Chinese hegemony, and an outer zone for those who did not.

"The hierarchical relationship between these zones was defined by the frequency with which tribute was presented to the emperor," explains Martin Stuart-Fox in *A Short History of China and Southeast Asia: Tribute, Trade, and Influence*. "In the central zone, this was on a daily basis in the form of produce and services rendered to the court. The [feudal] lords were required to present their tribute once a month, while tribute from the pacified zone was expected every three months. Controlled barbarians presented tribute annually, while those beyond, in the wild zone, were expected to appear only once at court, a symbolic appearance that signaled inclusion within the Chinese world order. . . . The tributary system . . . created clear distinctions between inner and outer barbarians, between those effectively colonized through imperial expansion, and those allowed independent status."

Accepting tribute was primarily a diplomatic ritual, rather than a way for the emperor to accumulate wealth. The tribute was considered a symbolic submission to Chinese superiority and power. In fact, the imperial court typically rewarded leaders who paid tribute with magnificent gifts, as a way to show outsiders the glory and might of the Middle Kingdom.

The Chinese emperors considered themselves "Sons of Heaven," so eventual control over the entire world was a political goal. A more critical reason for expansion was to provide security for the Middle Kingdom. Maintaining control over the inner zone of foreigners was vital to the Chinese strategy of creating reliable buffer states surrounding the Middle Kingdom, like a living Great Wall of China. These buffer states would fend off attacks by those living in the untamed fifth zone, and thus protect the Middle Kingdom.

Reasons for Muslim Expansion

By comparison, the Islamic empire developed from a combination of two powerful forces. One was a desire to spread the new religion; another was a growing feeling of Arab strength and solidarity, which created a desire to expand.

Initially, the Arabs who followed Islam were a small, weak community. Muhammad began to openly spread the message of his new religion in Mecca around the year 613. As he established a following over the next decade, the authorities in Mecca often persecuted Muhammad and the Muslim converts. By 622 the persecution had become so harsh that Muhammad and his followers took the drastic step of fleeing Mecca. The Meccans continued to attack even after the Muslims established their community in Yathrib (later called Medina). It was not until 630, when Muhammad and his followers had grown strong enough to subdue the

(Bottom) A decorated page from the Qur'an, the holy scriptures of Islam. (Top) A book of Hadith, the stories about Muhammad and his companion that complement the teachings in the Qur'an. These two sources are the basis for all Islamic law.

Meccans, that many Arab tribes were united under the banner of Islam.

One of the teachings of Muhammad was that Muslims should spread their new religion to others, so that eventually all mankind could join in submission to Allah. The theological simplicity of the new religion, and its clear set of rules for proper behavior, appealed to many Arab nomads.

However, warfare was also an important part of Arab culture. Muhammad had united some of the tribes through military alliances; other tribes had submitted to Islam after being defeated in battle. To support the growing numbers of Muslims, Muhammad and the subsequent Islamic leaders institutionalized ancient tribal traditions involving raiding parties. Arab armies were permitted to distribute the wealth gained from their raids, and collect taxes from subdued peoples. Hence, a precedent was set for the Islamic notion of empire as actively expansionist, born of equal parts religious fervor and warlike aggression.

Trade and Diplomacy

During his lifetime, the Prophet Muhammad spoke of China as the farthest reaches of civilization. The leaders who followed him were eager to make contact with China. The Tang dynasty learned about Islam, and the spreading Muslim empire, through trading contacts with Muslim Arabs.

A series of ancient trade routes across Asia had once facilitated trade between the Roman Empire and China. Rome had fallen centuries earlier, but the trade route between the Mediterranean Sea and China still bustled with caravans. (In the 19th century, a scholar named Ferdinand von Richthofe would call these routes the **Silk Road**, the name by which they are best known today.) In addition to the Silk Road, China traded with the west along two other land routes: from India through Tibet and Nepal; and from Myanmar (Burma) northeast through today's Yunnan province. Southern sea routes supplemented these overland routes. According to legend, in 616 Muhammad's maternal uncle, Abu Waqqas, joined a multi-year trading voyage that traveled from Ethiopia to Guangzhou on the South China Sea.

The first formal contact between the Muslim and Chinese empires is believed to have occurred through diplomacy. After capturing Byzantine territories in the Middle East, attacking the Persian empire, and establishing the Muslim capital in Damascus, the third Islamic caliph, Uthman ibn Affan, turned his attention to contacts with distant China. At the same time, the second Tang emperor, Taizong, who was directing China's expansion into Central Asia and Korea, decided that he wanted to learn more about the expanding Islamic empire in the Middle East. According to legend, in 650 Uthman sent Muhammad's uncle to the Tang court. By the time the Arab emissary arrived after a year of traveling, Taizong had died. He was succeeded by Emperor Gaozong, a sickly young man who preferred peace to war. The Sassanid Persian empire had fallen to the Arabs a short time earlier, and the royal family had fled into Chinese territory. Therefore, Gaozong was eager for conciliatory talks with the powerful Muslims.

Waqqas presented a copy of the Qu'ran and invited the Chinese emperor to embrace Islam. According to the Ancient Record of the Tang dynasty, Gaozong inspected the teachings of Islam and declared its precepts to be compatible with the teachings of Confucius. Chinese historians consider this event to be the birth of Islam in China. To show his approval of the new religion, the emperor provided money to construct China's first mosque in Guangzhou. This Mosque of Remembrance still stands today in the city, and is available to Muslims for prayer and to tourists for sightseeing.

According to Chinese records, between 651 and 798, as many as 39 official Muslim envoys visited China and many Arab and Persian Muslim traders and merchants relocated to China. The Tang government allowed foreign merchants to establish their own communities. Muslim traders were allowed to live in Guangzhou, Yangzhou, Quanzhou, Hangzhou, Kaifeng, and Luoyang. The most resplendent enclave of foreigners was in the Tang capital, Changan (Xi'an). Foreign diplomats and merchants were welcomed to this cosmopolitan capital. In addition to Muslims, the recorded population of over 5,000 foreigners included Hindus, Jews, Manicheans, Nestorian Christians, and Persian Zoroastrians. These diplomatic and business exchanges provided good conditions for Islam to spread within China through immigration.

War and Invasion

The Islamic and Chinese empires were not destined to remain at peace for long. The vast Central Asian steppe became the area over which the empires would contend. The Tang emperors had established friendly states (or *khanates*), ruled by the local king (or *khan*), along China's northern and western borders. These khanates managed the often-dangerous but lucrative trade routes and sent regular tribute to the emperor. Their main purpose was to protect China from invasion, as each buffer state fought to preserve control over its territory.

The Central Asian steppe is a unique region—thousands of miles of

The minaret of a mosque rises above Guangzhou. The first mosque in China was built in that city during the seventh century.

grassy, treeless prairie without natural boundaries or barriers. Nomadic tribes that were barely influenced by the civilizations around them populated this region. Both the Islamic and the Chinese empires saw expansion into Central Asia as furthering their imperial goals.

Between 630 and 640, the Tang pushed west to capture Kucha, Khotan, Kashgar, Yarkand, and Turpan. This established the area once called East (or Chinese) Turkestan, and today known as the Xinjiang province. By 659 the Chinese had pushed as far as Bukhara and Samarkand, important trading centers in modern-day Uzbekistan.

During the 640s and 650s, Islamic armies moved east into Central Asia. In 642 the Muslims defeated Sassanian Persian forces to gain control of eastern Iraq, and by 651 they had extended Muslim control over much of Persia (modern-day Iran) and captured the important city of Kabul, in Afghanistan.

In 669, Arab and Chinese armies clashed near Bukhara. Interestingly, this battle marked the first use of gunpowder in warfare, although the Tang rockets were used to make noise and frighten the Arabs' horses, rather than as lethal weapons. Nevertheless, the Arab forces continued to advance as far as Bukhara, from which they continued south to Basra (Iraq) and Khorasan (Persia). By 680, the Arabs had reached Samarkand, where they established a garrison. However, during the next century, Bukhara and Samarkand went back and forth between Islamic and Chinese control. By 700, less than 70 years after the death of Muhammad, Islam had spread to Balkh, in northern Afghanistan on the south branch of the northern Silk Road, and as far as the Pamir Mountains on the Chinese border.

In the midst of this turmoil, several Central Asian kingdoms composed of Turkic tribes emerged. These included the Turkmen in 683, the Uyghurs in 745, and the Kirghiz (today called the Kyrgyz) in 840. Over time, the members of these tribes adopted Islam, and Muslim culture and practices were assimilated into the traditional lifestyles of these Central Asians.

In 750, the Chinese captured and beheaded the King of Tashkent for rebelling against the emperor. This precipitated the Turkic Uyghurs to vacate

> **Chinese paper makers were among the prisoners captured by the Arab Muslims who conquered Samarkand. This was the beginning of the famous paper industry of Samarkand, from which the art of papermaking spread to the West.**

Inscriptions on Muslim tombstones in Guangzhou and other cities have helped scholars piece together the early history of Islam in China.

their alliance with the Chinese and to realign themselves with Arab forces. In July 751, a combined Arab/Turkic army decisively defeated the Chinese at the battle of Talas, northeast of Tashkent. The Chinese army had considerably outnumbered the Muslim forces, so their defeat was a psychological blow to the Tang rulers. Chinese expansion to the West ended, and the catastrophe precipitated a decline in Chinese military might. The victorious Uyghur kingdom came under increasing Islamic influence, becoming Muslim with the conversion of the Khan of Kashgar in 934 A.D.

Invasion of the Mongols

Two centuries later, under Genghis Khan, the Turkic tribes of the Mongolian steppe were united into a powerful empire. Genghis Kahn made an alliance with the Uyghurs, but he needed money to pay troops securing the northern frontier of Mongol territory. To get it, he decided to invade China. By 1217, the Mongols had crossed the Great Wall, conquered important cities of the Jin dynasty in northern China (including the capital, Beijing), and forced the Chinese to pay tribute to Genghis Khan.

For the last ten years of his life, Genghis Khan continued to conquer others. By the time of his death in 1227, the Mongols ruled a vast empire that

> Marco Polo (1254–1324) was a Venetian who traveled with a trade caravan to China during the 13th century. He arrived in 1275, as the Yuan emperor Kublai Khan was completing his conquest of China. He wrote a famous account of his journey, in which he described one settlement this way: "Lop is a large town at the edge of the Desert, which is called the Desert of Lop, and is situated between the East and Northeast. It belongs to the Great Khan, and the people worship Mahommet [sic]."

stretched from Beijing to the Caspian Sea.

It proved impossible for a single ruler to control the Mongol Empire as successfully as Genghis Khan, and by 1260 the empire was divided into four khanates. In the west, the ruler of what became known as the Persian khanate, Genghis's grandson Hulegü Khan, completed his conquest of the Arab Abbasid Empire, sacking its capital at Baghdad. This effectively ended Arab control over the Islamic empire. In the east, another of Genghis's grandsons, Kublai Khan, directed a Mongol invasion of southern China. The conquest of China's Song dynasty, which ruled southern China, took 16 years, ending in 1279.

The Mongol leader Genghis Khan (1162–1227) was one of the greatest conquerors the world has ever known. By the time of his death, he had established Mongol control over much of Asia.

Kublai Khan, and the other rulers of what became known as the Yuan dynasty (1271–1368) did not permit Mongols to assimilate with the Chinese. To rule the territory, the Mongols employed many educated Central Asian Muslims as administrators. One of the most important of these Muslims was Sayyid Adjall, who served as governor of what is now Yunnan, Sichuan, eastern Tibet, Guangxi, and much of north Vietnam. Although the Mongols were hated as outside conquerors, the Chinese observed the effectiveness of Muslim administrators. As a result, Muslims in China became more influential than their numbers would suggest.

The first Arab merchants who arrived in Xi'an built a mosque in the city more than 1,200 years ago. Today, the site of that orignal mosque is occupied by the Great Mosque of Xi'an, pictured here.

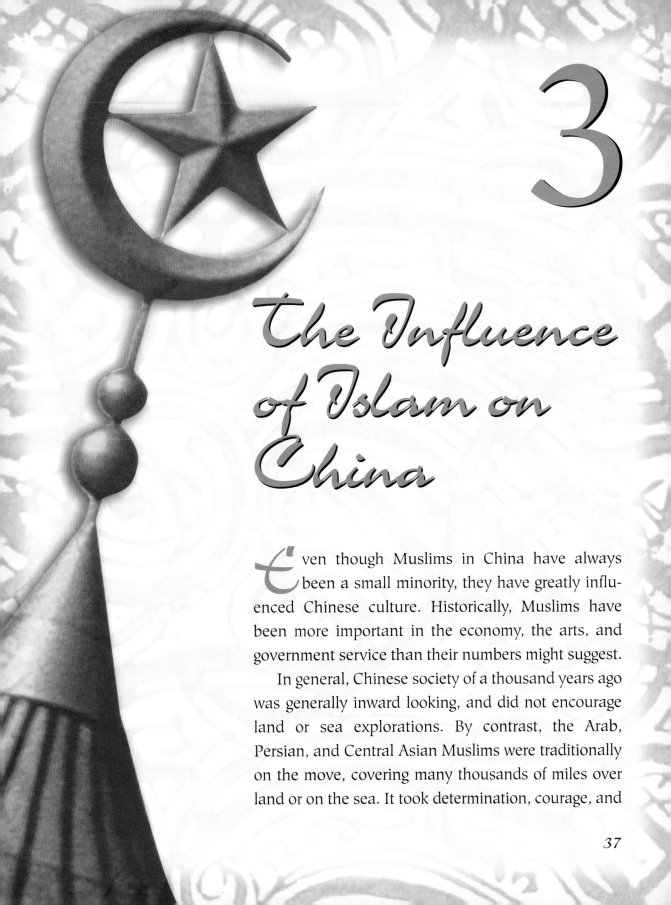

3

The Influence of Islam on China

ven though Muslims in China have always been a small minority, they have greatly influenced Chinese culture. Historically, Muslims have been more important in the economy, the arts, and government service than their numbers might suggest.

In general, Chinese society of a thousand years ago was generally inward looking, and did not encourage land or sea explorations. By contrast, the Arab, Persian, and Central Asian Muslims were traditionally on the move, covering many thousands of miles over land or on the sea. It took determination, courage, and skill to journey to China, because travelers faced many dangers. Long after the early Muslim immigrants had been assimilated into the dominant Han culture, the characteristics that had helped them survive the journey were reflected in their chosen professions—transportation, innkeeping, and soldiering. Even today Muslims are well represented in these work activities in modern China. But the area in which Muslims made the greatest mark—and which enabled them to exert a great influence over Chinese society—was as merchants.

In the Confucian hierarchy of imperial China, merchants were despised. They were considered low in status, well below craftspeople and peasant farmers and not much higher than slaves. Confucius believed that merchants were by nature exploitative, because they did not produce a worthwhile article or foodstuff, but accepted a portion of an item's value simply by acting as a middleman. He deemed this unproductive and unethical.

Because most Chinese wanted to avoid this despised trade, it was easy for Muslims and other non-Han traders to take over merchant activity without interference. In fact, Muslim immigrants were encouraged to handle trade in the Middle Kingdom. During the Tang (618–907) and Song (907–1279) dynasties, permission was granted for permanent Muslim merchant communities to be established in major cities as well as in the capital, Changan (near Xi'an). Foreign Muslims who settled permanently in China were even allowed to own land.

In these settlements, Arab and Persian Muslims led peaceful lives. They built homes, mosques, and cemeteries. Because the traders were men, and Islam encourages marriage, young single men found it practical to marry local Chinese women and start families in China. When Muslims married, their Chinese spouses were expected to convert to Islam, and their multi-ethnic children became the early Chinese Muslims.

The Chinese called these Muslims *Hui*, because most early Muslim traders expected to one day return to their homelands. The Chinese

A silk merchant displays his wares at a market in Kashgar. This city in western China was an important stopping point on the Silk Road, and today it has a large Muslim population.

character *Hui* means "those who will return." However, most Hui eventually gave up their plans to return, remaining in China and assimilating in many ways with their Han Chinese neighbors. (Today, to many Chinese people the word *Hui* has become synonymous with Islam, and is used to denote one of the larger Muslim groups within China.)

In general, these merchants followed their Islamic faith privately and tried to avoid conflict with the Chinese over cultural and religious issues. Most had come to China as traders, rather than as missionaries, so for the most part they did not overtly preach Islam to the larger Chinese community. Instead, they discreetly adapted to the predominant economic and cultural conditions in order to facilitate their merchant activity within China. As a result, the Han Chinese generally looked with favor on these useful and unobtrusive Muslim communities.

The number of Muslims in western China gradually increased through natural family growth, adoption of Chinese orphans, and occasional conversions. Immigration increased their numbers even more. Most permanent immigrants came overland to northern China from Central Asia along the Silk Road. These immigrants included soldiers, diplomats, scholars, artists, traders, and religious leaders. Some were employed by the Chinese government or military. Others established shops or acted as religious leaders in mosques that the Chinese Muslim communities had built.

Small Muslim communities also flourished in the coastal cities of China. In each important port, Muslim merchants purchased incoming ship cargoes and sent export goods for sale in other parts of the world. Unlike in western China, however, many of these commercial administrators did eventually return to their homes in Arabia or Persia, finding it relatively easy to come and go on the steady traffic of oceangoing Arab fleets.

Muslim Influences on Chinese Cuisine

Historically, Chinese cuisine was largely dominated by the influence of southern China. Meals primarily included rice with stir-fried leafy vegetables and bits of lightly seasoned seafood, poultry, or pork. As Muslims arrived in China, they brought a robust new cuisine. Unlike traditional Mongol or Tibetan cuisines, which never influenced Chinese cuisine to any great extent, the Muslim style of food preparation exerted a strong influence.

Because Islam forbids Muslims from eating pork, the spicy fare of Muslims often incorporated such meats as grilled lamb, goat, and beef. Xinjiang cuisine, which includes flat hearth-baked bread, wheat noodles, and grilled lamb, is especially popular in China. Because a Uyghur-style meal is generally dry and quite salty, it is typical to finish the meal with a broth soup instead of a sweet desert. In the Xi'an region and most of Sichuan province, the food served in restaurants as well as at street stalls is often hot and spicy. Chili peppers, which were introduced from Central America in the 1600s, are an important ingredient.

The origins of one of China's classic cuisines, the Bejing style, can be traced back to the Liao dynasty (907–1125). After the fall of the Tang, some of the tribal groups of northern China started to move south for protection from Mongol raiders. These Turkic groups, many of whom became Muslims, brought their style of food from northeastern China and the Mongol Plain to the city. After the Mongols conquered China and established the Yuan dynasty (1271–1368), the new imperial family soon abandoned the traditional diet of the Mongolian nomads: meat, mare's milk, and fermented yogurt. Instead, they developed a taste for Muslim and

Young Hui women prepare beef ribs at a stall in Xi'an. Because eating pork is forbidden by Islam, Muslims in China introduced different meats in their cooking.

An Uyghur baker sits behind stacks of flatbread.

Chinese-style foods, creating what today is recognized worldwide as a classic Chinese cuisine.

Muslims also brought a new standard of sanitation to China. Islamic traditions include *wudu*, or ritual washing before prayer. Muslim *halal* butchers and restaurants, which conform to Islamic dietary restrictions, still enjoy a reputation for high sanitary standards among non-Muslim Chinese and are patronized all over China.

Muslim Influences on the Arts

In the arts, some Muslim influences have been so thoroughly adapted by the Han that most people consider them Chinese. An example is the famed blue and white porcelain, which was first fired during the Yuan dynasty. For centuries the Muslims had been using cobalt to make blue and white tiles decorated with "arabesque" designs, a unique style of intertwining lines making a complex abstract form. These tiles were used to decorate mosques throughout Persia, Syria, Iraq, Arabia, and Afghanistan. The Chinese, who were expert porcelain-makers, traded with Muslims in the Middle East for the cobalt to make blue glazes. The used it to create exquisitely designed vessels, tiles, plates, and vases utilizing a variety of designs.

Muslims also introduced decorative metalworking techniques to China. During the early Ming dynasty (1368–1644), Muslim traders introduced the art of cloisonné to Chinese metalsmiths. Cloisonné is the fusing of enamels with designs made from copper wire over a copper base. In Chinese hands, cloisonné became a unique art form. Intricate and brilliant cloisonné objects are still produced and sold to collectors and tourists today. Another technique involved inlaying gold designs in steel. This became known as damascening, because it originated in Damascus. During the Qing dynasty (1644–1911), Chinese sword makers used this technique to decorate steel blades.

The impact of Islam on the architecture of China can be seen particularly in the design of mosques. In some areas, Muslims simply converted Buddhist temples into places where they could worship Allah. In those cases, they often built a low, wide minaret tower outside the temple, from which a mosque leader would call the faithful to prayer. In urban areas, new mosques were generally built using the traditional Chinese architectural style. Inside, panels with quotations from the Qu'ran in both Chinese and Arabic calligraphy were hung on the walls and prayer rugs placed on the floor. In remote rural villages, however, Muslim Chinese often built their mosques following the classical Middle Eastern style—pointed arches, slender minarets, and plain white

This porcelain vase dating from the Yuan dynasty features dragon, phoenix, cloud, and floral motifs. The Chinese adapted the use of cobalt glazes from Muslims, who had long used them to make decorative colored tiles.

exteriors. Today, tourists who visit these village mosques are often amazed by the structures, which look as though they belong in Syria or Persia, rather than the Chinese countryside.

In music, the two-stringed Chinese instrument *erhu* is derived from the Persian *kamanche*, which made its way to China with Muslim traders through Central Asia during the Song dynasty. The *kamanche* is a instrument similar to a violin, with a round sound box. It is held upright and the horsehair bow is drawn horizontally over the four strings to make the sound. In the Chinese version of this instrument, the *erhu*'s round resonator is covered with python skin, which creates a unique whining sound, and the player draws the bow between the two strings, rather than across them. In a Chinese orchestra, the *erhu* is considered to produce the sound closest to a human voice.

Muslims in China's Government and Military

Chinese Muslims often played important military roles, often as hired mercenaries, for the imperial Chinese governments. Muslim leaders in the buffer states were powerful individuals and were able to mobilize large numbers of soldiers on very short notice. When organized around a strong leader, members of different clans and ethnic groups could be welded into a formidable fighting force. Muslim soldiers soon gained a reputation for being well disciplined and courageous fighters, and they often served in the most important regiments of imperial troops.

The seafaring skills of Arab Muslims were instrumental in defending the Song dynasty from attack during the 12th century. Early in the century the Jin attacked the Northern Song dynasty, and in 1126 captured the Song capital at Kaifeng. The Song emperor escaped south and set up a new capital at Hangzhou; thereafter, this became known as the Southern Song dynasty. However, the new southern capital was vulnerable to attack from the sea—pirates and invaders could easily sail up coastal rivers to besiege the city. The Southern Song court worked with the local Muslim seafarers to convert their merchant vessels, which were armed against pirate raids, into a makeshift navy of armed warships. Eventually, the Song built naval shipyards where they constructed specialized warships. To pay for the new navy, Muslim merchants were encouraged to resume their lucrative overseas trade, which brought tax revenues to the Song government.

During this time the Chinese learned many of the skills of navigation and shipbuilding from Muslims. Throughout the period of Southern Song rule (1127–1279), they established Chinese trading communities on many islands of the Malay and Indonesian archipelagos, as well as the Indian subcontinent. These distant communities were the beginnings of what were to become today's "overseas Chinese"—ethnic Chinese who retained their traditional culture and world view, but who lived permanently outside the sphere of direct imperial rule. Many of the traders who lived in these communities were Muslims, and their efforts helped spread the religion to Java, Sumatra, and the Malay peninsula. This contributed to the Islamization of much of Southeast Asia. Today, Indonesia has the world's largest Muslim population at more than 205 million, while Malaysia has become a leading country in the Muslim world.

The Mongol Yuan dynasty (1279–1368) further established Muslim importance to Chinese public service. The great Mongol emperor Kublai Khan recognized that China was too rich a prize to wantonly plunder. Instead, Kublai sought to rule China pragmatically, employing trusted foreigners rather than conquered Confucian scholars to administer the Middle Kingdom. Muslims were especially favored in the Yuan court. Their discipline, organization, and effectiveness in battle transferred equally well to handling the vast projects undertaken in Mongol China. When Kublai Khan decided to build a new capital within China at Beijing (the closest major Chinese city to the Mongolian capital, Karakorum),

الفرآن ثم رابع اساطير بلادها ورخارف جلّدها وقال اركبوا فيها بسم الله مجراها

ومرساها ثم نفّس نفس المغرمين او عباد الله للكربين وقال اما انا

**The *dhow*, pictured in this illustration from an 11th century Arab manu-
script, was a sturdy sailing ship that Muslim traders used to bring goods to
and from China.**

Muslim architects and builders were commissioned to design and construct government buildings. Muslim doctors were employed as professors at the new Imperial Academy of Medicine. Central Asian Muslim traders were commissioned to carry on the lucrative trade along the Silk Road, and the paper money and promissory notes written and accepted all over the Muslim and Chinese world were written in Arabic and Uyghur, as well as Mongolian and Chinese.

The Mongols, as outsiders, were never fully accepted by the conquered Chinese, and when they were forced from power by the Ming dynasty in the 14th century, the Muslims in China suffered heavily. The Hui were forced to assimilate into traditional Chinese culture more rapidly than in any other period. This was particularly true of the Hui in Yunnan and in the northern areas of China. Many of them had originally been of Mongol, Turkic, or another ethnic background but embraced traditional Han culture to survive.

Many Muslims who had attained high office under the Mongols either fled or were killed. For example, the descendants of Sayyid Adjal, an influential Muslim administrator during Mongol times, disappeared from China under the rule of the Ming. Other Muslims changed their names. Some adapted Chinese names such as Mo or Ma for Muhammad, Mai for Mustafa, or Hu for Hussein. Many Muslims abandoned Arabic surnames altogether; often, when a Muslim married a Chinese woman he would simply take his wife's family name.

Despite this persecution, Muslims in China still made important contributions to politics, science, and the arts. Perhaps the best-known Chinese Muslim of the Ming dynasty was the explorer Zheng He, who commanded seven important voyages between 1405 and 1433. According to ancient Chinese chronicles, each voyage included more than 300 ships—many of which were said to be more than 400 feet long—and over 28,000 men. During these voyages Zheng He became the foremost ambassador of his time, visiting at least 37 countries and negotiating tribute and trade agreements with local rulers on behalf of the Ming emperor.

Despite Zheng He's successes, however, imperial advisors believed the voyages were wasteful. They argued that the Middle Kingdom produced everything it needed, and that the resources used to build and provision

The Life of Zheng He

The Muslim navigator Zheng He (1371–1435) has become one of the most famous Muslims of Medieval China. He was born Ma He in Yunnan. His family was descended from an early Mongol governor of Yunnan and a ruler of Bukhara. Both his grandfather and father had made the traditional Muslim pilgrimage to Mecca, so Ma He grew up hearing their accounts of travel through foreign lands.

Yunnan was one of the last strongholds of the Mongol Yuan dynasty, which was being forced from power in China by a peasant revolt led by Zhu Yuanzhang. When Ma He was 10 years old, Zhu Yuanzhang's army conquered Yunnan. The young boy was among 1,000 Muslim boys who were captured, castrated, and forced to join the army.

When Ma He was 19 years old, he was placed under the command of Zhu Di, the Prince of Yan. Ma He distinguished himself as a junior officer, skillful both in war and diplomacy, and eventually became a court eunuch of great influence.

In 1402, Zhu Di assumed the Ming throne as Emperor Yongle. Yongle restored Chinese prosperity, and then sought to display its power overseas. When Ma won a critical battle at a village called Zhengcunba, the treasure fleets should instead be redirected to the army, to defend against the Mongols or other threats to China's borders. An accidental fire that destroyed much of Beijing was considered a sign from Heaven that the sea voyages had been a mistake for the new dynasty. As a result, the Ming dynasty abandoned the potential of its explorations. Most of the fleet's records were destroyed and the building of oceangoing ships was

Emperor Yongle gave him the new surname Zheng, to commemorate the victory. He later chose him to command the naval missions, even though Zheng He had never been to sea before.

Zheng He's first voyage began in 1405. The fleet visited Champa (South Vietnam), Siam (Thailand), Malacca (now part of Malaysia), and Java (an Indonesian island), then crossed the Indian Ocean to the ports of Calcutta, Cochin, (both of which are in India) and Ceylon (Sri Lanka). When he returned to China in 1407, he brought a great deal of treasure. He returned from another voyage in 1415 with the envoys of 30 kingdoms in southeast Asia, who wished to visit the Ming court. Other voyages spread the fame of China and the Ming emperor.

In 1424 Emperor Yongle died, and his successor, Emperor Hongxi, suspended the naval expeditions. Zheng He was ordered to disband the fleet. However, in 1431 Zheng He was given permission to make one last voyage. During this trip he visited kingdoms in southeast Asia, the coast of India, the Persian Gulf, the Red Sea, and the east coast of Africa. During this journey, he also made the ritual pilgrimage to Mecca that is required of all Muslims. Zheng He returned to China in the summer of 1433 and died two years later.

The Muslim navigator Zheng He is believed to have made several remarkable seafaring trips for the Ming emperor between 1405 and 1433. This Chinese wood block print depicts one of his enormous ships.

banned for a time. However, China continued to participate in a seagoing trade with Indonesia, India, East Africa, and other countries in the region.

In the centuries that followed, European explorers would sail to all parts of the world. They would establish colonies in Africa, America, and finally in the nations of East Asia. Some scholars argue that because China had halted its program of exploration and global trade so early in the modern era, the country would suffer and eventually be humbled by the stronger European colonial powers.

A Hui man stands outside a pavilion in Lanzhou. The Hui are Muslims who, for the most part, have assimilated into Chinese culture. Other than their religious practices, the Hui are Chinese in most respects.

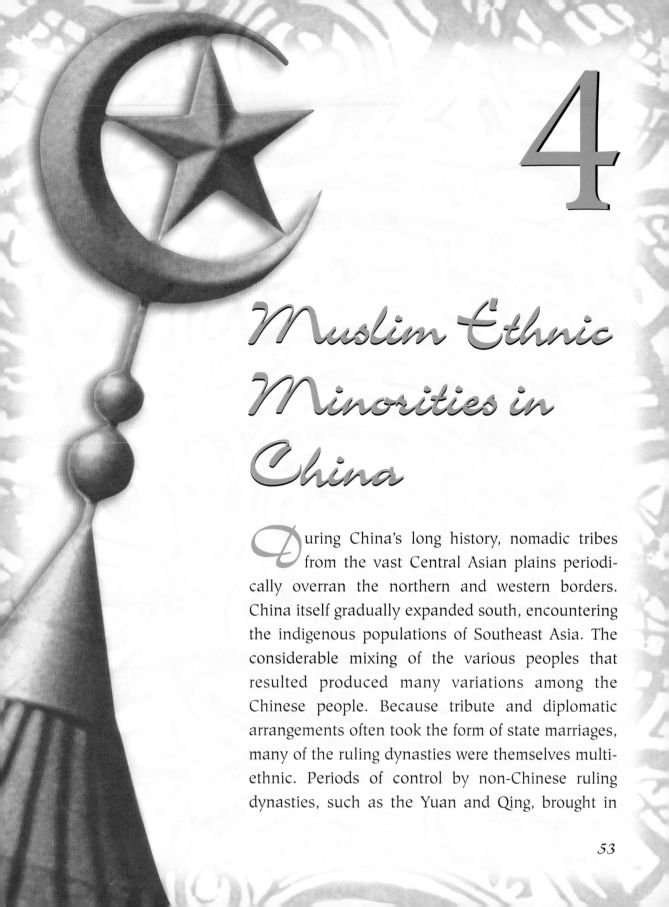

Muslim Ethnic Minorities in China

During China's long history, nomadic tribes from the vast Central Asian plains periodically overran the northern and western borders. China itself gradually expanded south, encountering the indigenous populations of Southeast Asia. The considerable mixing of the various peoples that resulted produced many variations among the Chinese people. Because tribute and diplomatic arrangements often took the form of state marriages, many of the ruling dynasties were themselves multi-ethnic. Periods of control by non-Chinese ruling dynasties, such as the Yuan and Qing, brought in members of many other ethnic groups: Mongols, Turks, Afghans, Arabs, and Persians.

By the early 20th century there were many different peoples in China, but no one had a clear idea of what the different groups were, or how many people were members of each group. In the 1920s Sun Yat-sen, the founder of the Republic of China which replaced the imperial system of government after 1911, called his country a "republic of five nationalities"—Han, Hui, Mongol, Manchu, and Tibetan. Chiang Kai-shek, who led the Guomindang (Nationalist) government during the 1930s and 1940s, claimed that China had no ethnic minorities; all people in China were sub-branches of the Han Chinese, the group that makes up most of China's population. During the 1950s, after the communist People's Republic of China was established, China's leader Mao Zedong decided that a scientific survey was the best way to properly answer the ethnic question. When ethnic groups were invited to register with the government, more than 400 different groups responded.

As Chinese government officials sorted through these registrations, they decided that many of those who thought of themselves as different nationalities were actually members of a single ethnic group. To clarify the issue, the government sent anthropologists and historians all over China to investigate. The Chinese government chose to define an "ethnic nationality" as a group of people of common origin living in a common area, using a common language, and having a sense of group identity in economic and social organization and behavior. By 1957, the Chinese government officially recognized 55 ethnic groups (including the majority Han) as independent nationalities living in the country. The number of nationalities changed several times over the next few decades, until in 1994 the State Ethnic Affairs Commission ruled that the government would not recognize any new ethnic groups. Today, there are 56 official ethnic groups in China.

According to the 2000 census, the Han make up 92 percent of China's population; the minority groups combine for about 8 percent (about 106 million people). Approximately one-fifth, or 20 million, of these minority peoples are Muslims.

The two largest Muslim groups are the Hui and the Uyghurs. The Hui can be found all over China, and are descended from the various Muslim traders who came to China over the years and integrated with the Han Chinese. Other than their religious beliefs, in many ways they are practically indistinguishable racially and culturally from the Han. The Uyghurs are a Turkic group with physical characteristics that are distinctly different from the Han Chinese. They also have significant cultural differences.

For most of their history, the Uyghurs lived as tribes in a loosely affiliated nation on the northern Chinese border (sometimes called East Turkestan). Most do not think of themselves as Chinese, and some want to break away from China and form an independent state. They wish to emulate their Turkic Muslim neighbors in Central Asian states like Kyrgyzstan, Uzbekistan, and Turkmenistan, which gained independence in 1991 after the collapse of the Soviet Union.

Other officially recognized Muslim groups in China are racially Mongol, Tibetan, Indo-European, or Turkic. In addition, there are some Muslim groups that are not officially recognized by the government. Many of these smaller ethnic groups are considered to be part of one of the larger groups, even though their language and culture may be different. An example is the Aynu, a group of about 6,200 Muslims who speak a language derived from Persian. Because the Aynu live among the Turkic Uyghurs (whose language is Altaic), they have been classified by the government as Uyghurs.

The Hui

The Hui are the largest Muslim group in China, numbering 9.1 million according to China's fifth national census, conducted in 2000. Large groups of Hui live in the Ningxia Hui Autonomous Region, which is located in northwest China. This is one of five autonomous provinces within China. Large Hui communities can also be found in Xinjiang, Gansu, and Qinghai. The so-called "scattered Hui" live in nearly all Chinese cities. Beijing is home to approximately 200,000 Hui, while 150,000 Hui live in Tianjin and 50,000 Hui live in Shanghai.

The Hui differ from other Chinese Muslim groups in that they do not speak their own language. Instead, they speak the dialect common where they reside, often sprinkling their conversations with a handful of Arabic or Persian words such as *salaam*, a greeting of peace used by most Muslims.

Most Hui are **Sunni** Muslims who follow the Hanafi school of Islamic jurisprudence, which offers a moderate interpretation of the religion. However, there is a wide range of adherence to Islamic practices among the Hui, depending on where they live. In northwestern China most Hui are quite conservative and follow Islam strictly. In Beijing and the coastal cities, many Hui are more liberal in their religious practice.

The Hui have retained their ancient aptitude for trade, and today many are employed in small business working leather, making jewelry, and trading wool. Others work as *halal* butchers, providing meat that has been slaughtered according to the requirements of Islamic law, or operate *halal* restaurants where noodles are served with grilled beef and lamb. The rural Hui of northern China grow wheat while Hui farmers who live farther south raise rice. Many also raise sheep and cattle, and grow vegetables for sale as well. Most urban Hui are laborers and factory workers in the big state industries.

In rural communities where the entire village is Hui, the traditional clothing of Hui men includes a white or black skullcap and a black vest over a short white gown. The Muslim leaders and teachers often wear a distinctive green overcoat. In the past, Hui women wore a scarf that covered

A man rides through the fertile Gansu region. A large Hui population can be found in Gansu, a province in the northwest of China that borders Xinjiang.

The Niu Jie Mosque in Beijing was built in 997, making it the oldest of the city's more than 65 mosques.

their hair and shoulders entirely but left their faces visible. Today, older Hui women wear a black or white headscarf, while young women and unmarried girls wear white caps or brightly colored scarves over their hair.

In areas where the Hui live together with members of other ethnic groups, they generally adopt the local dress. For instance, Hui in Diqing dress like other Tibetans, while Hui women in Xishuangbanna wear narrow-sleeved blouses and funnel shaped skirts that are nearly the same as those worn by Dai women. Hui who live in urban areas often dress the same way that the Han Chinese do; for young Hui, this generally means the t-shirts and jeans that other young Chinese wear every day.

The Uyghurs

Unlike Hui Muslims, who over time intermixed with the Han Chinese and were assimilated into their traditional culture, the Uyghurs remain a separate ethnic nationality. They are descended from Turkic peoples of the Altai Mountains. Over time, some Turkic tribes migrated throughout central and western Asia, where during the 20th century their descendents would establish such modern countries as Turkey, Uzbekistan, Kazakhstan, Kyrgyzstan, and Turkmenistan.

The ancestors of the Uyghurs were Turkic nomads who lived near Lake Baikal in southeast Siberia. They established a powerful kingdom in Central Asia around A.D. 745, but by 840 they were forced to flee their homeland by raiders from another tribe, the Kyrgyz. Moving south, they settled near the Silk Road trade routes, in what today is the Uyghur Autonomous Region of China's Xinjiang province. The people called themselves Uyghur, which means "united" or "allied," and established kingdoms around such cities as Turpan. The independent Uyghur kingdoms fell to the Mongols during the 13th century. After the Mongols conquered China, Uyghurs served as valuable "foreign" administrators and workers for the Yuan dynasty. Because the Uyghurs lived along the Silk Road, many became involved in trade.

Like the Hui, most Uyghurs are Sunni Muslims who practice the moderate Hanafite form of Islam. Uyghur religious practices are greatly influenced by **Sufism**, a mystical branch of the religion in which devotees believe they can draw closer to God through special spiritual disciplines, such as ritual chanting or ecstatic dancing.

Today, there are more than 8.4 million Uyghurs living in China's Xinjiang province. Some farm the desert oases, where they grow melons, cotton, corn, peaches, plums, and wheat. Uyghurs also live in the picturesque Tian Shan mountain range, where they live primarily as herders. In urban areas

Uyghurs pray together in a mosque. Most Uyghurs follow Sunni Islam, although their religious rituals and beliefs are heavily influenced by Sufi practices.

like Urümqi and Kashgar, Uyghurs have developed industries such as manufacturing, mining, and oil drilling. Overall, the Uyghurs are relatively prosperous compared to other minority groups in China.

Uyghurs wear loose clothing with brightly colored patterns. In the past, most Uyghur women wore bright, broad-sleeved, one-piece dresses topped with a black vest. The modern Uyghur woman wears Western style clothes except on special occasions. Uyghur men often wear a long gown with a belt but no buttons.

Uzbeks, Kazakhs, and Kyrgyz

In addition to the Uyghurs, smaller numbers of other Turkic ethnic groups live in China today. The largest of these groups are the Kazakhs, who number about 1.3 million.

An Uyghur girl wears a silk headdress and a brightly patterned traditional dress.

Other Turkic groups include the Kyrgyz (171,000) and Uzbeks (14,000).

Although there are few Uzbeks in China, they are one of the largest Turkic groups in Central Asia. In ancient times the Uzbeks lived along the Silk Road; the name *Uzbek* derives from a powerful ruler of the 14th century who converted to Islam and encouraged his people to convert as well.

Today, most of the Uzbeks in China live in Yining, although there are significant Uzbek communities in Qoqek, Kashgar, Urümqi, Yarkant, and Kargilik. Most Uzbeks live in nuclear families, in which parents live with their small children, without other relatives sharing the household. Like most Muslims, Uzbeks respect education, and as a result many young people become teachers. Other Uzbeks living in China are traders or work in handicraft industries. In general, the Uzbeks living in urban areas are extremely well educated and are among their cities' elites. However, the same is not true of the few Uzbeks who farm and raise livestock in rural areas.

Both Uzbek men and women wear brightly embroidered skullcaps. Women often cover the cap with a headscarf. The men wear knee-length robes, which are decorated with colorful embroidered lace. These robes are held together with a wide embroidered belt. Men wear sturdy dark colored boots. The women wear colorful loose pleated dresses without waistbands and brightly embroidered boots trimmed with felt or fur.

Uzbeks are also famous for their folk music and dancing. Uzbek dances have very fast steps and involve spinning motions. Usually the dances are performed solo, with the dancer wearing traditional Uzbek costume.

The Kazakhs are a group that broke away from the larger Uzbek group during the 15th century. According to their folklore, Kazakhs believe they are descended from a fierce horseman who was famous for terrorizing travelers on the Silk Road; in fact, the Turkic word *kazakh* means "profiteer." Today, most of the Kazakhs in China live in the western Xinjiang province, which borders the modern state of Kazakhstan. Other Chinese Kazakhs live in Gansu and Qinghai provinces.

About one-third of Kazakhs are nomadic herders who migrate seasonally, searching for fresh pastures for their sheep and goats, and in some cases cattle or horses. During the summers, Kazakhs live in yurts, large tents made by stretching thick felt over wooden poles. In the winter months, when they are staying in one place, they live in simple houses made of adobe or cement blocks. Most Kazakhs, however, live in urban areas. Like the Uzbeks, these Kazakhs are generally very well educated and often hold important positions in integrated communities.

Kazakh horsemen race on a grassy track near Yining. The horse is an important part of traditional Kazakh culture.

Unlike the Uzbeks, however, most Kazakhs hold unorthodox religious beliefs. The Kazakhs converted to Islam by the 16th century, but over the centuries they incorporated elements of traditional steppe religions, such as ancestor worship and **shamanism**, into the way they practice Islam.

The Kyrgyz are a nomadic people who live on the western edge of China near the borders of Kyrgyzstan and Tajikistan. Some nomads still herd livestock through the high country of Xinjiang, but most live more settled lives in towns and villages. Overall, Kyrgyz culture is closer to that of the Kazakhs than it is to the Uzbeks or Uyghurs. Like the Kazakhs, the Kyrgyz have developed a syncretistic form of Islam. The Kyrgyz are not as well educated as Kazakhs or Uzbeks, and in general they are less prosperous than other Muslim groups in China.

Kyrgyz men wear blue or black sleeveless long gowns made of sheepskin, camelhair, and in summer, cotton cloth. This outer robe is worn over

A group of Kazakh women wear colorful clothing. These women live in the Tian Shan Mountains of China.

a white embroidered shirt and leather trousers. From their leather belts Kyrgyz nomads often hang a flint (for making fire) and a small sharp knife. They wear sturdy leather boots. Kyrgyz women wear a wide collarless jacket and black vest over a red long dress. They embroider their boots, and wear silver chains in their hair. Both men and women wear a small dark corduroy skullcap over which they place a high-topped leather hat called a *terai*. Sometimes a woman will wear a bright headscarf over her cap as well.

Tatars and Dongshiang

Several of China's minority groups were formed by the intermarrying of Turkic and Mongol peoples. These include the Dongshiang, who number about 400,000 in China, and the Tatars, who number about 5,000.

Dongxiang Muslims are of mixed Mongolian and Turkic descent; their ancestors settled on the outskirts of Hezhou during the rule of the Yuan dynasty. Many served the Mongol rulers as soldiers, and after the Yuan fell they remained in China, settling in river valleys and becoming subsistence farmers. The Dongxiang generally refused to intermarry with the Han Chinese, and therefore preserved their racial characteristics. Today, the Dongxiang primarily live in a long valley of the Gansu province. This region is generally arid and quite rocky. Until relatively recently, it was illegal for foreigners to visit this area; even though tourism is now permitted, outsiders only rarely see this remote and culturally protected valley. However, because the Dongxiang are so isolated, they are among the poorest Chinese minorities, and generally have substandard housing, health care, and education.

The Dongxiang are devout Muslims. About two-thirds are Sunni Muslims, while the remainder are Shiites. Each Dongxiang village has at least one mosque, and Linxia, the main city of the region, is sometimes called the "Mecca of China" because it has so many mosques.

The Dongxiang are primarily farmers. They grow potatoes, wheat, barley, millet, and corn. They use a basic potato mash to make snacks, alcoholic drinks, and noodles. Men wear robes with buttons down the far left and a broad waistband. On the waistband they hang knives, snuff bottles, and small bags for carrying things. They wear a sort of beret cap, a white shirt topped with black vest, and dark trousers. In winter, they wear sheepskin coats. Dongxiang women wear embroidered outfits, which include shirts with wide sleeves and decorated trousers. Older women wear kerchiefs and young women wear colorful embroidered cotton caps and silk veils. For special occasions, they wear embroidered shoes with a medium high heel.

The Tatar ethnic minority in China is the product of nearly a thousand years of Turkic and Mongolian tribal mixing. Some Tatars traded with the

Chinese during the Tang dynasty, while others are descended from the Mongol Golden Horde of the 14th century. However, most of the Tatars in China today arrived during the 19th century. When Russians forced them from their lands along the Volga River, the Tatars migrated to the Xinjiang province. Most Tatars live in the cities of Urümqi, Taiqing, and Yining.

During the late 19th century, Tatar clerics opened schools in the cities and rural areas of Xinjiang. These schools focused on study of the Qu'ran, Islamic law, and history, but they also taught arithmetic, science, and the Chinese language. These schools provided the first organized education system for Muslims in the province, and were open to any Muslim living in Xinjiang, not just Tatars.

Tatars in China are known for their intellect, education, and rich culture. They are very musical and dances are accompanied by folk versions of wooden flutes, harmonicas, accordions, mandolins, and a two-stringed instrument like a violin. Men use squatting, kicking, and leaping motions in the vigorous dances. Tatar men often wear an embroidered white shirt and black trousers under a black robe, and a black curly fur or black and white embroidered cap. Women wear white, yellow, or purple pleated skirts and a small black pearl-decorated cap set forward on the head, with a short veil attached that covers the rest of the head and neck. Some Tatars have begun to wear Western style clothes.

The Salar and Bonan

Most of China's approximately 90,000 Salar Muslims live in the Xunhua Salar Autonomous County in Qinghai province, although smaller groups live in Gansu province. According to their legends, the Salar came to this region from Samarkand in the 13th century. After being defeated by enemy tribes, two brothers who are considered the ancestors of the Salar set out from Samarkand with a white camel and a copy of the Qu'ran. When they came to Qinghai, their camel wandered off while they were

A bilingual stop sign in Xinjiang, written in Arabic and Chinese.

sleeping. When the brothers found it, the camel had turned to stone. They considered this a sign to settle there.

Over time, the Salar intermarried with Hui, Tibetans, and Han Chinese. Their Turkic-based language borrows many Chinese and Tibetan words. Until relatively recently, their language was not written; today, some Salar write using Chinese characters.

The Salar converted to Islam during the late 17th and early 18th centuries. They have remained deeply religious and are reputed to be among the most zealous Muslims in China. This has contributed to tensions with China's government. In 1958, when Mao Zedong feared that the Salar and other Muslims were inciting revolt, the government removed all of the

This enormous statue of Mao Zedong looms over a courtyard in Kashgar. In 1949, Mao established the People's Republic of China; the Communist Party continues to rule the country today.

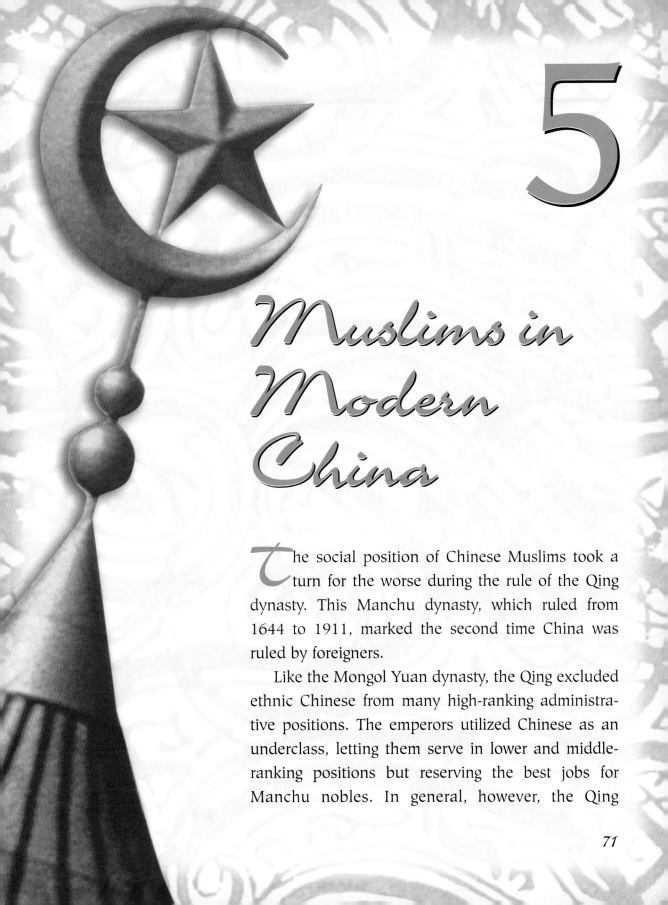

5

Muslims in Modern China

The social position of Chinese Muslims took a turn for the worse during the rule of the Qing dynasty. This Manchu dynasty, which ruled from 1644 to 1911, marked the second time China was ruled by foreigners.

Like the Mongol Yuan dynasty, the Qing excluded ethnic Chinese from many high-ranking administrative positions. The emperors utilized Chinese as an underclass, letting them serve in lower and middle-ranking positions but reserving the best jobs for Manchu nobles. In general, however, the Qing admired Chinese civilization, and as rulers they strove to understand and replicate Chinese ways. (Some said that the Qing were "more Chinese than the Chinese.") The Qing emperors demanded that their subjects conform to Chinese traditions. This policy was sometime forced on minority groups, which followed their own cultures and traditions.

Muslims in China resisted attempts to suppress their non-Chinese ethnic identity and heritage. Some groups tricked the Qing by claiming that they were Mongols, because the Mongols had been Qing allies in their conquest of China. Other Muslims attempted to withdraw completely from traditional Chinese culture.

The Qing also found it advantageous to incite hatred among Han Chinese toward "outsiders," whether they were Muslims or members of other ethnic or religious backgrounds. The Qing used this "divide and rule" strategy to distract the Han Chinese, so they would be less likely to unite and rebel against the Manchu rulers. Increasingly, Chinese Muslims were besieged as a result. This unfortunate Qing policy is one reason for the antagonism today between some Han Chinese and some Chinese Muslims.

Movements within Islam to change the way the religion was practiced also caused stress within the Chinese Muslim community. During the 18th century, various reform movements emerged. Most of these insisted on a more rigid interpretation of the Qur'an and replacement of the syncretic practice of Islam with stricter adherence to traditional Islamic law. Soon Islamic reformers were changing the ways in which Chinese Muslims practiced their religion.

Schools of Sufi reformers soon implanted new ideas among Muslims in China, particularly among the Hui in Gansu. Before the 18th century, the Hui had externally integrated to Chinese culture, while remaining personally true to Islam—a popular saying of the Hui was, "Muslim indoors, Chinese outdoors." However, over the years some elements of Chinese culture had become mixed into the Hui practice of Islam. The reformers inspired many Hui to reclaim their Muslim differences—to feel that being true to Islam was more important than blending into Chinese society.

A Muslim Sufi teacher named Shah Naqshband inspired two main reform movements, which evolved in very different directions. The Khuffiya Naqshbandi advocated isolation from worldly society and stressed private prayer and such rituals as veneration of the Muslim saints. The Jahriyya Naqshbandi, by contrast, advocated active—even militant—political involvement in worldly affairs and a return to strict adherence of the practices followed by Muhammad and the first generation of Muslims.

There was so much friction between the different Muslim reform groups in China that bloody battles sometimes erupted. Some of these evolved into uprisings against the Qing overlords. The Qing had reclaimed Muslim Xinjiang in 1759 from the remnant of the Mongol Empire, and did not want any trouble with the Chinese Muslims in Gansu. They executed Ma Mingxin, founder of the Jahriyya Naqshbandi order, in 1781, and attempted to outlaw Muslim reform movements from that point forward.

Eventually, the Qing emperor became the arbiter of disputes about doctrine between different Chinese Muslim groups. This set a dangerous precedent in which the secular government determined the legitimacy of religious practices for the various Muslim groups. The Qing emperors were not impartial judges; their rulings generally favored the group that was aligned more closely to imperial China's needs. The Qing also used their authority to suppress unruly Hui Muslims.

During the mid-19th century, Muslims saw Qing losses in a series of engagements with European powers (known as the Opium Wars) as a sign that the imperial grip over China was weakening. During the Taiping rebellion, which lasted from 1855 to 1873, sympathetic Muslims revolted unsuccessfully in Yunnan. A more successful separatist movement emerged in Gansu a few years later, when Hui Muslims launched the Northeast Hui Rebellion of 1862–76. This succeeded in separating Gansu temporarily from the failing Qing Empire, and opened the way for another breakaway movement, a Uyghur rebellion in Xinjiang from 1864 to 1877. In all there were five major conflicts involving Muslim rebels during the last half of the 19th century, and these were put down by the Qing only after great difficulty.

Another major factor causing stress between Muslims and Han Chinese during the late Qing dynasty was an explosion in China's population. In a relatively short period, the Chinese population tripled, increasing from 100 million in 1650 to 300 million by 1800. The introduction of new crops from the Americas during the 16th and 17th centuries, such as peanuts, potatoes, corn, and sweet potatoes, was an important contributor to the population growth. These crops could survive in poorer, drier soils or on hillsides unsuitable to traditional Chinese crops, making more food available to feed the growing population. In fact, a Chinese farming manual written around 1625 suggested planting sweet potatoes as a form of insurance—even if a drought caused a famine, the sweet potato plants would still yield enough food to prevent outright starvation.

However, as the population grew, the cities and farmland became too crowded. Because the Qing forbade any Han Chinese to relocate to fertile Manchuria, large numbers of Han Chinese migrated instead to the lands on the frontiers of China where many Muslims lived. This contributed to tension between the newcomers, who wanted the land, and the Muslims who had lived there for generations. The Qing quelled disputes quickly and with force, generally siding with the Han and oppressing the Muslims.

Overthrow of the Imperial Government

During the second decade of the 20th century, the rulers who controlled much of Asia—the Russian czar and the Chinese emperor—were overthrown. In Russia, unrest forced Czar Nicholas II to abdicate in March 1917 and a republic was formed; later that year, the Bolshevik Revolution led to a civil war that ultimately resulted in the creation of the Union of Soviet Socialist Republics (U.S.S.R.). In China, the nationalist leader Sun Yat-sen and others successfully rebelled against the Qing dynasty in 1911, and replaced the corrupt and decayed imperial bureaucracy with a new republican government in 1912.

Sun Yat-sen's intended his government to be organized around five equal "nations," including the Muslims as one group. The Hui in particular began to organize Muslims from the many regions of China, and established numerous political, charitable, and educational organizations between 1912 and 1934. Some of these national Muslim organizations still exist today in China.

An armed member of the Chinese revolutionary society Fists of Righteous Harmony—better known as the Boxers. In 1900, the Boxers rose up in protest against Western commercial and political influence in China. During the rebellion, the Empress Cixi encouraged Muslims from Gansu to fight with the Boxers in Beijing.

Between 1916 and 1927, however, the nationalist government fell apart and China collapsed into a period of warlord rule over smaller

The Chinese revolutionary leader Sun Yat-sen proclaimed that China belonged equally to five groups: the Han, Hui, Manchu, Mongols, and Tibetans.

provinces. Two groups joined forced to defeat the warlords and reunite China, the Chinese Communist Party (CCP) and the Guomindang (GMD). However, once the Guomindang, under Chiang Kai-Shek, was in power it turned on the communists and tried to eradicate them. This resulted in a civil war that lasted more than 20 years.

For Muslims, life under the Guomindang government was not much different than it had been under the imperial government. Chiang Kai-Shek believed there were no separate ethnic groups in China, merely different strains of Han Chinese. Nevertheless the Muslim press became vigorous, and printed periodicals were eagerly read and discussed by Chinese Muslims. Muslims in China were concerned about defining their cultural identity and place within the Chinese world.

During the late 1920s and 1930s, China became a safe refuge for Muslims fleeing the Soviet Union, where Joseph Stalin was directing persecution of Kazakhs, Kyrgyz, Tajiks, and others he considered a potential threat to the Soviet government. Hundreds of thousands of people were killed during these purges. As a result, many Central Asian Muslims crossed the border to enjoy relative peace in China.

Because of the Soviet persecution, many Muslims in China supported the Guomindang government during its civil war with Chinese communists. However, some Hui joined the communist cause after the Long March by Mao Zedong and his followers in 1934. The March ended in the Shaanxi province, near Yan'an, where the communists could hide out in the caves. In the guerilla war, which began after the Long March, many Hui from west of Yan'an, led by the powerful warlord Ma Hongkui of Ningxia, joined Mao's communist followers. These Hui Muslims were the only minority group to join with the communists in sizable numbers during China's civil war.

By October 1949, the communists had emerged victorious, and Mao Zedong established the People's Republic of China (PRC). Chiang Kai-shek and his followers—including about 20,000 Muslims—fled to the island of Formosa (Taiwan), where they continued to insist that theirs was the legitimate Chinese government. However, the Communist Party now held control over mainland China.

In the early years of the PRC, some Muslims fared well under Mao Zedong's policies. Mao rewarded the Hui Muslims who had helped the communists win the civil war by establishing the Ningxia Hui Autonomous Region. This was consistent with a PRC policy regarding ethnic minorities that was similar to Stalin's method of defining and politicizing the U.S.S.R.'s ethnic minorities by placing them in "autonomous" republics.

The Chinese government attempted to scientifically define and elevate the various ethnic minorities residing in China. Fifty-four minority nation-alities were identified and autonomous ethnic political regions were designated for the larger groups. One of the aims of the PRC was to encourage Muslims to identify with their ethnic roots and not with pan-Islamism, a movement that had developed in the early 20th century that called for all Muslims to be united under the rule of a caliph, or religious leader. Such a movement threatened the secular states of Asia by chal-lenging the PRC's control over its citizens.

There were some problems, however. The PRC appointed Muslim governors of the various Muslim autonomous regions. The Han Chinese who lived in these areas as minorities resented being ruled by Muslims. Also, during the 1950s the communist government instituted a policy of

Mao Zedong, pictured here voting in a 1953 People's Congress election, encouraged the classification of Chinese ethnic minority groups.

collectivization of agriculture. Traditionally, Hui and Han Muslims had avoided tension by living in separate villages; however, under the new system all the villages in an area were administered together as a single commune, and all of the people were expected to work together. There were tensions over the shared work (some Han believed certain Muslim ritual practices, such as stopping during the work day to perform the required prayers, were unfair interruptions) and other issues (such as eating pork, which the Han prefer and the Hui shun).

Overall, however, Muslims were largely ignored by the central government. In some ways, communist social reforms improved the lives of many Muslims, especially the women. Traditional Islamic practices like child marriages and polygamy were outlawed, and women were given the same divorce and inheritance rights as men. The PRC helped Muslim farmers economically as well, sponsoring irrigation projects to improve agricultural output. Tragically, this time of relative peace would soon be shattered.

Muslims during the Cultural Revolution

In the mid-1960s, Mao Zedong felt his power waning. To regain his tight grip over the Communist Party, Mao and his associates unleashed a movement to "purify" the party by eliminating capitalist influences. Intellectuals, liberal party leaders, and anyone suspected of harboring capitalist or non-communist thoughts was arrested and executed or sent to brutal prison camps called "re-education centers." This movement, which lasted from 1966 until Mao's death in 1976, became known as the *Cultural Revolution*.

The Red Guards, an organization made up mostly of students, provided the shock troops of the Cultural Revolution. The Red Guards were empowered to destroy any architecture or art that reflected pre-Communist Chinese corruption or Western capitalistic decadence. This included anything created or written prior to 1949, so their "smashing"

Young Red Guards, carrying a picture of Chairman Mao, chant Communist Party slogans as they march down a street. The Cultural Revolution, which lasted from 1966 to 1976, claimed millions of victims and turned Chinese society upside-down.

campaign resulted in incalculable destruction of China's cultural heritage.

The Cultural Revolution actively targeted Muslims as a non-conforming group. Mosques and schools were destroyed, and the government forbade the teaching of Arabic, which is required to properly read the Qu'ran. Long-standing Chinese intolerance to outside differences made Muslims easy targets. Some Han Chinese, particularly those who lived as

The story of how Hui Muslims saved their Great Mosque in Xi'an from the marauding Red Guards during the Cultural Revolution is fascinating. Each night Muslim men would come to the mosque armed with sharp sabers. They would fill as many buckets of water as they could, then turn down the lights, lock the walled gates, and wait in the darkness of the inner courtyards, armed with their knives and surrounded by their water buckets. On many nights, they needed to put out fires started when gangs threw homemade fire-bombs over the courtyard walls. However, word soon spread that armed Muslims waited inside the walls, so throughout the Cultural Revolution the Red Guards never dared to personally scale the walls and attack the mosque. Thanks to the Muslims' diligent guard, the Great Mosque in Xi'an survived relatively undamaged.

minorities in autonomous regions ruled by Muslims, saw the Cultural Revolution as an opportunity to pay the Muslims back for slights both real and imagined. Crowds cheered as Muslims were forced to eat pork and to renounce their faith or else be beaten to death by the rabble. Hundreds of thousands of Muslims were killed during the Cultural Revolution.

Ultimately, however, the Cultural Revolution was a horrible time for most Chinese, and devastated an entire generation spiritually, educationally, and economically. After Mao's death subsequent Chinese leaders condemned it as a misguided policy and imprisoned, tried, and executed the leaders of the movement, who were known as Gang of Four. Deng Xiaoping and other leaders who followed Mao also implemented numerous reforms that continue to affect China's government and economy today.

China's Deng Xiaoping and U.S. President Jimmy Carter sign diplomatic agreements, January 1979. The U.S. decision to grant formal recognition to the communist government of China opened the way for normal trade relations between the two countries.

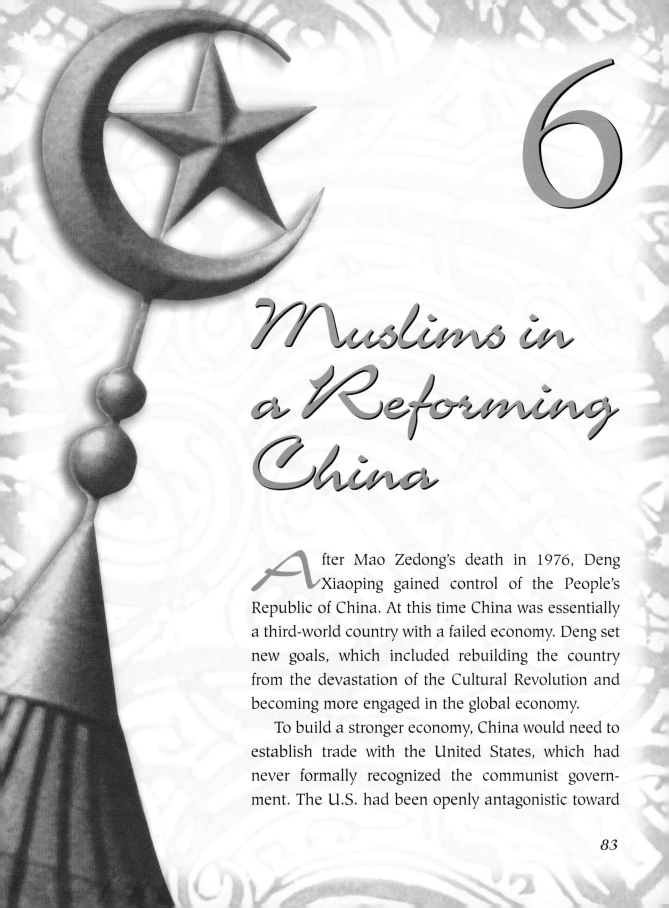

6

Muslims in a Reforming China

After Mao Zedong's death in 1976, Deng Xiaoping gained control of the People's Republic of China. At this time China was essentially a third-world country with a failed economy. Deng set new goals, which included rebuilding the country from the devastation of the Cultural Revolution and becoming more engaged in the global economy.

To build a stronger economy, China would need to establish trade with the United States, which had never formally recognized the communist govern-ment. The U.S. had been openly antagonistic toward

Red China during the 1950s and 1960s, but in the early 1970s relations between the two countries began to improve. In February 1972 U.S. President Richard M. Nixon made an historic visit to China; at the end of his visit, Nixon and Chinese Premier Zhou Enlai issued the Shanghai Communique, which stated that both countries endorsed the goal of normalizing relations. In 1979, the United States formally recognized the People's Republic of China, and relocated its embassy from Taipei, Taiwan, to Beijing.

In 1980, China was awarded Most Favored Nation (MFN) trading status by the United States. A country designated Most Favored Nation is not forced to pay restrictive tarrifs on products it imports to the U.S. Without

U.S. President Richard Nixon meets with Mao Zedong in February 1972.

MFN, it is virtually impossible to trade effectively with the United States. The U.S. extends MFN status to all but a handful of countries; in fact, in 1998, the name for this status was changed to Normal Trade Relations (NTR), because it is the norm rather than a special benefit. In nearly all cases, once MFN (or NTR) is granted, the status is permanent. China was a special situation, however. The U.S. government decided that China's trade status should be evaluated and approved or denied each year. In this way, the United States could pressure the Chinese government to improve its record on human rights.

During the Cold War, China had been criticized by the West for its invasion of Tibet, for the excesses of the Cultural Revolution, and for its crackdown on political dissent. In an effort to show the world that China was committed to reform, a new constitution was written in 1978, then revised and adopted in 1982. In the constitution, the people of China were promised specific rights and freedoms.

Because of China's economic reforms, by the end of the 20th century the country's gross national product, a measure of economic activity, was growing at greater than 8 percent a year. Within the once-classless communist society, millions of people were being added to a prosperous middle class. However, political reforms did not keep pace with the economic changes. International watchdog organizations such as Human Rights Watch and Amnesty International catalogued numerous incidents of Chinese oppression throughout the 1980s and 1990s. Sometimes, dissenters attracted global attention, as was the case with student demonstrations in Tiananmen Square during the spring and early summer of 1989. The Chinese government was internationally criticized for its harsh response to the demonstrators.

Despite Tiananmen and other incidents, the United States continued to annually grant Most Favored Nation trading status to China. With its population of more than a billion people, China is an enormous market for U.S.

A view of Tiananmen Square, where in 1989 a government crackdown on student demonstrators drew international condemnation.

businesses, which lobbied Congress to continue to extend the status. In 2000, the U.S. government established permanent Normal Trade Relations with China, eliminating the need for an annual review of the status.

Since 1996, the Chinese Information Office has published so-called "white papers" for international audiences, describing progress on human-rights issues in China. According to these publications, in recent years the Chinese government has focused on improving conditions for its minority Muslim groups. However, most western experts feel the country has a long way to go on human rights.

Protection under the Constitution

China's 1982 constitution assured minority peoples of equality, and promised government assistance in meeting their special needs. Article four of the constitution states, "All nationalities in the People's Republic of China are equal." According to the constitution, the state is not permitted to discriminate against or oppress any nationality, and must protect the rights and interests of each nationality within China. At the same time, however, the constitution clearly states that attempts by the minority groups to break away from China is illegal: "Any acts that undermine the unity of the nationalities or instigate their secession are prohibited."

Today national minorities do enjoy some special government benefits. They are exempt from China's "one-child" policy, which was established to slow the growth of the population. As a result of this, the population growth rate among Muslims and other minority groups was significantly higher than among the Han Chinese, according to data from the 2000 census. Other benefits for minority groups included lower test score requirements for admission to secondary schools, special tax breaks, and government subsidies. The government permits minorities to speak their own languages, and recently a cellular phone system that supports the Uyghur language was installed in Xinjiang.

Chinese nationality policy has become more sensitive when it comes to official names of minority groups. Although a 1951 legislative decree abolished discriminatory appellations for minorities (such as the Chinese word for "pig" which was formerly used for the Yi minority), the Han rulers selected most of the minority group names. Today, the ethnic minorities are referred to by the names they choose to call themselves. For example, before the 1980s the Chinese referred to Dongxiang Muslims as Mongolian Huihui, meaning Eastern Village Mongolians. Even place names have been changed, as when the Chinese city Dihua reverted to its earlier Muslim name, Urümqi.

The Chinese government has taken steps to help Muslims meet their religious obligations. Government regulations require cities and towns with significant Muslim populations to have a certain number of Muslim restaurants. Large businesses offer separate Muslim dining areas and prayer rooms, and Muslim factory workers are given time off to celebrate

The Red Hill Pagoda looks out over the Chinese city of Urümqi. The city was renamed Dihua after the PRC was established, but during the 1980s the Chinese government changed the name of the city back to its original Muslim designation.

their religious holidays. Beef and mutton supplied to Muslims is slaughtered and processed according to Islamic customs. Mosques are exempted from property taxes, and some famous mosques have been renovated with government funds. The government also pays for the training of new religious leaders. Muslims can be married by their mosque's imam, rather than by a government Marriage Officer, and they are permitted to bury their dead (Chinese custom calls for cremation).

Despite the government's efforts, much remains to be done. Critics point out that career opportunities in state-sponsored factories and lucrative political jobs are not evenly distributed.

Implicit, but not stated, in article four of the constitution is that only members of ethnic minorities groups who have registered with the government are granted special constitutional rights. When the new constitution was ratified, some minorities waited to register because they were uncertain whether the benefits promised to them would actually happen, or if registration would simply target them for new persecutions. By the 1990s, however, it was clear that the government would honor its promises. As a result, registration of minorities increased and many smaller groups petitioned the government to also be recognized as separate minority nationalities.

Religious Freedom in China?

Communist ideology is atheistic. It denies the existence of God and teaches that religion is a tool used by powerful capitalists to distract the worker from his or her inequal condition. However, the 1982 Constitution promises freedom of religion to all Chinese. According to article 36 of the constitution, "Citizens of the People's Republic of China enjoy freedom of religious belief. No state organ, public organization or individual may compel citizens to believe in, or not to believe in, any religion; nor may they discriminate against citizens who believe in, or do not believe in, any religion. The state protects normal religious activities."

In reality, however, article 36 and other specific laws actually define the government's control over religious practice in China. The government recognizes five religions as legitimate: Islam, Buddhism, Taoism, Catholicism, and Protestant Christianity. The state has established religious organizations to oversee the activities of the various religious groups. These include the Islamic Association of China, the Buddhist Association of China, Taoist Association of China, Chinese Patriotic Catholic Association, Chinese Catholic Bishops' College, Three-Self Patriotic Movement Committee of the Protestant Churches of China, and the China Christian Council. All mosques, temples, and churches must register with the appropriate religious association, and the government can shut down non-registered congregations. Critics assert that the government monitors participants' activities and ideas through these organizations.

One reason the Chinese government registers and regulates religious adherents is to discover and eliminate potentially subversive activities before they can take root. Article 36 states that religious bodies in China cannot be subject to any foreign domination—for example, Chinese Catholics must obey the government, not the Pope. In the case of Chinese Muslims, the spread of the fundamentalist movement known as Islamism during the past three decades has made this prohibition more relevant. Some Islamists support the concept of a super-state composed of all Muslims, governed by the Qur'an and Islamic law, similar to the earlier pan-Islamic movement.

The government considers any religious belief system other than the accepted five to be a cult. Membership in a cult is a criminal act in China, and the punishment can be severe. In some cases, such as the Kaifeng Jewish community, minority religious groups are struggling to be identified as an ethnic minority for protection against the cult law. Other groups, such as Falun Gong, are suffering persecution by the authorities.

Improving Conditions for Muslims

During the Cultural Revolution, mosques were often defaced, destroyed, or closed. Today, mosques have not only been reopened, but many have been rebuilt with central government funds. Today there are more than 30,000 active mosques in China, with over 40,000 clerics serving the approximately 20 million Chinese Muslims. That is, on average, one cleric per 500 believers. Every year, the government allocates specialized funds for the maintenance and repair of major mosques. For example, in 1999 7.6 million yuan (almost $1 million U.S. dollars) was given by the central government to the Yanghang Mosque in Urümqi, the Baytulla Mosque in Yining, and the Jamae Mosque in Hotan. Today, the Great Mosque in Xi'an is undergoing major repairs, the first stage of which, renovation of the *minbar* (a mosque's pulpit), will cost about $179,000.

A Chinese mosque leader holds a copy of the Qur'an; behind him is distinctly Chinese artwork depicting Mecca and the Kaaba.

Because the rampaging Red Guards also destroyed copies of the Qu'ran, the Chinese government paid to have new copies of the holy scripture printed. Enough copies were printed that mosques could sell the extras to Muslims who had lost their copies in the Cultural Revolution. By 1997 there were some eight different translations of the Qu'ran from Arabic into Chinese, Uyghur, and other languages.

Today, Islamic literature can be found quite easily throughout China. Newspapers, books, television programs, and films are produced in the many languages of the various Muslim ethnic groups. The *Xinjiang Daily*, for example, is published in Uyghur and Kazakh as well as in Chinese. In the past 25 years, the Xinjiang regional office in charge of the collection and publication of ancient books and languages has preserved more than 5,000 titles. More than 100 ancient books have been translated into modern Uyghur or Chinese languages and published, including two colossal works, *Kutadgu Bilig* ("Wisdom of Fortune and Joy") and *A Comprehensive Turki Dictionary*, which was originally composed during the Karahan Kingdom period in the 11th century.

Minority students today are able to go to schools where they are taught in their own languages, and are also allowed to take university entrance examinations in their own languages. Public schools generally do not include religious training, so Muslims must learn about Islam at home, by reading books, and through their local mosques and religious colleges.

Tourism, one of the key economic strategies of China's government, promotes Muslim ethnicity. Not only are outside tourists bringing foreign currency, but Han Chinese are showing increased curiosity about these different peoples from the "outer empire." Routinely, a reader of *China Daily* will see cultural and entertainment notices and reviews, such as advertisements for festivals in the Muslim district of Beijing, or shows by the "minority marvel" Uyghur Song and Dance Ensemble. Local tourism offices often offer short excursions for urban Chinese to visit the distant locales. In 2001 alone, the province of Xinjiang, with its unusual natural scenery and colorful Muslim ethnic minorities, hosted over 8 million Chinese tourists. The government is also taking special pains to preserve and promote the colorful sports, folk dances, and songs of the Muslim minorities.

In recent years, growing numbers of Chinese Muslims have been permitted to make the **Hajj**, or ritual pilgrimage to Mecca. Muslims believe one of the great benefits of the *Hajj* is the exchange of ideas with Muslims from all over the world. In 1986, some 2,300 Chinese Muslims were permitted to make the *Hajj*. (In the same year, just 30 Soviet Muslims were allowed to make the pilgrimage.) Today, the number of Chinese Muslims going to Mecca each year exceeds 20,000. However, the government still keep tight control over who is allowed to participate in the *Hajj*.

Chinese Muslims have been allowed to make peaceful protests to further their cause, and have been rewarded by the government when they have sought to correct injustices through the legal system. For example, in 1996 Muslims staged a massive protest rally in Beijing to demand the removal of anti-Islamic literature from China's bookstores. In 1997, the government moved to ban the literature, which it said violated the Chinese Muslims' constitutional rights.

In recent years, the Chinese government has increased its spending on the Muslim areas of China. A recent white paper issued by the Chinese Information Office reports, "Since the beginning of 2004, funds for helping the poor provided by the Central Government [have been] increased by 60 million yuan ($7.5 million U.S.) to be used primarily in programs for invigorating the border areas, [helping] the poor [and] accelerating development in border areas inhabited by ethnic minorities. . . . Beginning in the autumn of 2003, the central and local governments jointly earmarked funds to provide textbooks free of charge to poverty-stricken students at the stage of compulsory education in 56 counties of Xinjiang, and exempted them from

A class of Muslim students studies their lessons in Urümqi. In recent years the communist government has permitted Muslims and other ethnic minorities to attend schools in which they are taught religious and cultural traditions.

all school fees. . . . Some cultural relics in . . . Xinjiang Uyghur Autonomous Region have been repaired."

This renewed focus on Muslim minority groups, particularly poorer groups like the Kyrgyz and Dongxiang, and on improving life in the border regions, is a clear sign that the government is more willing than ever before to accommodate and help its Muslim citizens. Improving the lives of Chinese Muslims has several benefits for the government as well. Perhaps one of the most important benefits is that better conditions in Xinjiang will help to reduce support for the Uyghur separatist movement in that province that has been battling to break away from China for decades.

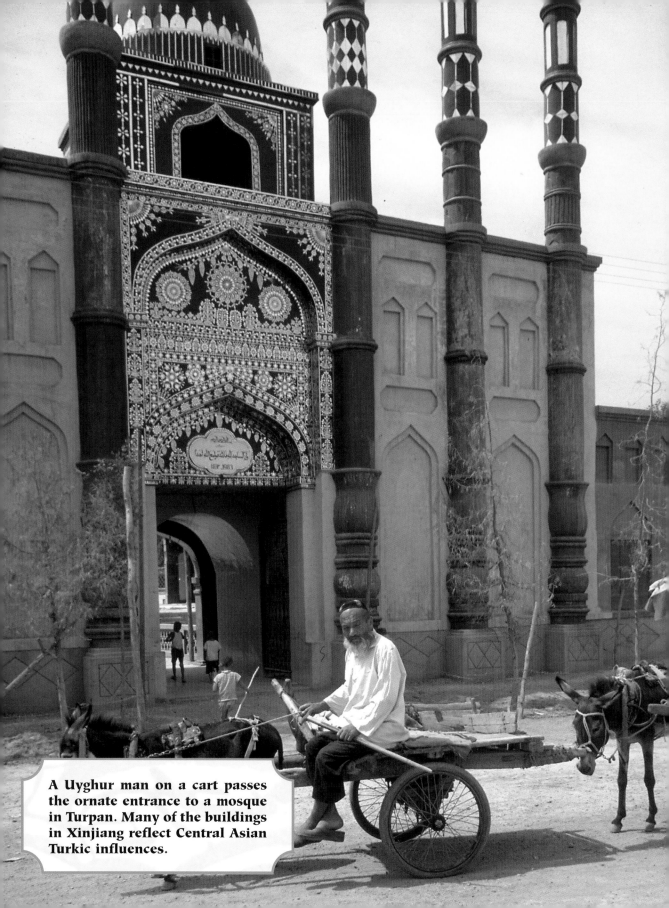

A Uyghur man on a cart passes the ornate entrance to a mosque in Turpan. Many of the buildings in Xinjiang reflect Central Asian Turkic influences.

7

The Uyghur Separatist Movement

For centuries, the vast Xinjiang province, which comprises one-sixth of China's total area, has been a true crossroads of Central Asia. As ancient tribes entered the region sometimes known as Turkestan, some settled while others moved on. Empires established outposts, and camel caravans passed through bearing valuable trade goods. In this highland desert interspersed with occasional oases, a strong tribal leader might control one or more small communities. These leaders would know their counterparts in other oasis regions of the desert, but none could force the others to be subservient.

Over time, the tribes of Turkestan pledged their allegiance to outside rulers—Chinese, Mongols, Uzbeks, Uyghurs, and others. In 1759, the armies of China's Qing dynasty captured East Turkestan from the Mongols. The Muslims of East Turkestan were restless under the Qing, however, and rebellions were common throughout the 19th century. In 1866, under a military leader named Yakub Beg, East Turkestan briefly regained independence from China. Yakub Beg ruled from Kashgar, where he established a government based on conservative Islamic principles. The independent state lasted until 1877, when Yakub Beg was killed and the Qing regained control. After this, the Qing renamed the region Xinjiang, meaning "New Frontier."

After the Qing Empire fell in 1911, most Chinese Muslims in Xinjiang switched allegiance to the new Republic. However, when the Soviet Union was formed, its leaders did not want a strong Chinese presence on their eastern border. They encouraged the Muslims of Xinjiang to revolt against the Chinese. At the 1921 Tashkent Conference, the Soviets assembled all the tribal leaders of Western Xinjiang, and suggested that the ancient ethnonym "Uyghur" be resurrected and applied to all non-nomadic Turkic people of the region. With Soviet help, the Uyghurs established a short-lived East Turkistan Republic in 1931. Although the Chinese re-conquered this state by 1934, the Uyghurs broke away again ten years later. This time, they were more successful and remained independent from 1944 until 1949, when East Turkestan was folded back into the newly formed People's Republic of China.

Long Struggle for Freedom

In 1951, the PRC "liberated" another frontier region, Tibet. Its leader, the Dalai Lama, escaped to India and began a long and compelling public relations campaign against Communist China in the West. Almost immediately, the Uyghur leaders who had escaped to the West made

A lone man rides past the ruined walls of Gaochang. This ancient Uyghur city-state flourished in Xinjiang between the ninth and thirteenth centuries.

secret contact with the Dalai Lama. The Uyghurs believed their causes were identical—like Tibet, they argued, East Turkestan had been an independent nation until it was cruelly invaded and occupied by the People's Republic of China. The Uyghurs worked in the West to free their homeland, which they called Uyghuristan, from China. Secret communications supporting the struggle were smuggled to Uyghur relatives back in Xinjiang.

The communist government, naturally, took a different view of the separatists' struggle. During the Cold War, China found itself in an uneasy position between the Soviet Union and United States. The government considered all separatists—like the Taiwanese nationalists, the Tibetans, and the Uyghurs—as treasonous citizens who were aligning with the West against China. The following is taken from an official government description of the struggle in Xinjiang:

> In the early 20th century and later, a small number of separatists and religious extremists in Xinjiang, influenced by the international trend of religious extremism and national chauvinism, politicized the unstandardized geographical term "East Turkestan," and fabricated an "ideological and theoretical system" on the so-called "independence of East Turkestan" on the basis of the allegation cooked up by the old colonialists. They claimed that "East Turkistan" had been an independent state since ancient times. . . . They incited all ethnic groups speaking Turki and believing in Islam to join hands to create a theocratic state. They denied the history of the great motherland jointly built by all the ethnic groups of China. They clamored for "opposition to all ethnic groups other than Turks" and for the "annihilation of pagans," asserting that China had been "the enemy of the 'East Turkestan' nation for 3,000 years." After the "East Turkistan" theory came into being, separatists of all shades raised the banner of "East Turkistan" to carry out activities aimed at materializing their vain wish of establishing an "East Turkistan state."

Until the early 1980s, little was heard about the Uyghur separatist movement. The Chinese government believed that the Uyghurs, like the Hui, would eventually become assimilated into Han culture if there was greater contact between the two groups. Consequently, social and economic programs were created that would force this to happen.

One early social program in the People's Republic of China was the encouragement of large families. During the 1950s and 1960s, this caused a population explosion, which created overcrowded conditions in the settled areas of eastern China. Because more than 60 percent of

China's territory is settled by its minority groups, who make up less than 10 percent of the total population, the Chinese government encouraged Han Chinese to migrate to the border regions, such as Xinjiang, where they could develop the resources of those regions for the state.

To make the westward migration more attractive, the Chinese government established economic-development programs in Xinjiang. The province is home to many valuable natural resources, including China's largest oil and gas reserves. Soon, non-Muslim workers were moving from the overcrowded cities to take new factories and large collective farms in Xinjiang. This influx of Han settlers greatly changed the composition of Xinjiang and other autonomous regions. For example, in the 1950s more than 90 percent of Xinjiang's population was Uyghur. The Han population of the province was less than 5 percent. Today, Uyghurs make up less than half of the population (47 percent), while the percentage of Han Chinese has risen to 37 percent.

To prevent tension between the Han settlers and the established Muslim groups, the trend has been toward tighter government administration. At one time, the government permitted local tribal leaders or imams to rule with only loose supervision, as long as there was no trouble. During the 1980s, however, the central government decided it needed greater involvement to most efficiently manage and exploit the resources of the frontier lands. The Uyghurs now complain that their province is autonomous in name only.

As a result of these changes, in recent decades the conflict in Xinjiang has intensified. Although the Chinese government tries to prevent Western media from getting information about its activities in Xinjiang, news organizations have recorded killings of dissidents and other human-rights violations. In April 1990, for example, government forces reportedly killed some 50 Muslim protestors when putting down a five-day uprising by religious extremists in Baren, south of Kashgar. When this uprising was followed by

Uyghur Muslims meet outside of a mosque.

other outbreaks of unrest throughout Xinjiang, the authorities, for the first time, admitted that the separatists were responsible. Since then, there have repeated reports of bombings and assassinations in urban centers in Xinjiang.

Attacks against Chinese soldiers and officials, as well as against perceived pro-Beijing Muslim sympathizers, continued in Xinjiang through the 1990s, and there were numerous reports of government forces making mass arrests of suspected separatists. Uyghurs complain that Islamic books, including copies of the Qur'an, have been destroyed by government officials and that they face discrimination in education and jobs. They also wish to make contact with Muslims outside of China, which they say is prohibited. In response, the government accused the East Turkestan Islamic Movement (ETIM) and other Uyghur separatist groups like the Eastern Turkistan Liberation Organization, the World Uyghur Youth Congress, and the East Turkistan Information Center of involvement in more than 200 acts of terrorism between 1990 and 2001.

The Separatist Issue Today

The September 11, 2001, terrorist attacks that destroyed the World Trade Center in New York and damaged the Pentagon near Washington, D.C., had an important affect on the Uyghur separatist movement. After the attacks, the administration of U.S. president George W. Bush launched a "war on terrorism" that targeted al-Qaeda, an international militant Muslim organization that was suspected of planning and carrying out the attacks. The U.S. also began cracking down on other Muslim extremist groups suspected of terrorism, and provided money to allies to stop terrorism. After repeated requests by China, in 2002 the U.S. government declared the East Turkestan Islamic Movement a terrorist group.

This was a controversial move. Terrorism experts disagree about the extent of the East Turkestan Islamic Movement's terrorist activites, or its links to al-Qaeda and global terrorism. The official U.S. government explanation was that new information indicated links between the movement and al-Qaeda. However, government critics have speculated the U.S. was pressured to designate the ETIM a terrorist group in exchange for better relations with China and support in the United Nations for U.S. military activities in Iraq. No matter what the reason, however, the official desig-

A Chinese Communist Party official gestures toward a display of weapons seized from East Turkestan Islamic Movement separatists. They were being shown as part of an anti-terrorism exhibit in Hotan.

nation gives the Chinese government a pretext to quash dissent among the Uyghurs of Xinjiang; all dissenters can now be lumped together as "terrorists" and prosecuted by the state.

Because of the restrictions that China places on both its domestic media and Western news agencies, no one is sure how widespread the Uyghur separatist movement is, or whether the Uyghurs are really a threat to China's control over Xinjiang. Most Western experts do not think the separatists are really a threat to Chinese control. They say the groups are too small and spread over too vast an area to wage an effective campaign for independence. However, some argue that Beijing's harsh response to the Uyghurs is actually creating more of a problem. These experts agree that unrest among the Uyghurs has increased, but they believe that not all of the Uyghurs want to separate from China. While some would like full independence, they say, other Uyghurs just want greater autonomy and better protection from human-rights abuses and discrimination. But China's heavy-handed approach may push greater numbers of Uyghurs into the arms of the Islamists, and actually increase the armed resistance.

The Uyghur separatist movement will certainly remain a major issue for China's government. Over the next few years, the growing Muslim population of China, as well as Muslims from around the world, will watch carefully to see how the Chinese government resolves the dispute in Xinjiang.

A.D. 622   The Prophet Muhammad leads his followers from Mecca to Yathrib (Medina), where the first Muslim community is established.

651   The Tang Emperor approves Islam as being compatible with Chinese beliefs and provides money for the construction of a mosque in Guangzhou.

751   Muslims defeat a larger Chinese army at the Battle of Talas. This important battle ends China's westward expansion and sets a longstanding border between the Chinese and Islamic empires.

1279   Rule of the Mongol Yuan dynasty over China begins. For the next century, the Mongol rulers hire Muslims as soldiers and administrators.

1368   The Ming dynasty comes to power in China. During its rule, which lasts until 1644, Muslims in China are forced to assimilate rapidly into the dominant Han culture.

1405   The Muslim admiral Zheng He sets out on his first voyage from China. The explorer would make several voyages, the last in 1433.

1644   The Manchu Qing dynasty takes control of China from the Ming. During Qing rule, which lasts until 1911, Muslims in China are often oppressed.

1759   The Qing gain control over East Turkestan from the Mongols.

1764   Under Yakub Beg, East Turkestan breaks away from China. The capital of the new independent state is located at Kashgar.

1877   East Turkestan is recaptured by China and renamed Xinjiang.

1912   The last Qing emperor abdicates, and the Republic of China is established by Sun Yat-sen and other nationalist leaders.

Chronology

1949   Mao Zedong founds the People's Republic of China (PRC) on October 1.

1957   The Chinese government officially recognizes 55 ethnic groups (including the majority Han) as independent nationalities.

1966   The Cultural Revolution begins; lasting for a decade, the revolution targets Muslims and others accused of betraying the principles of Chinese communism.

1972   President Richard Nixon makes an historic visit to China, opening the possibility of normalized relations and global trade between the PRC and the U.S.

1980   China is granted Most Favored Nation trade status, although a waiver requires that its status be evaluated annually as a way to force China to improve its record on human-rights issues.

1982   China's new constitution, which includes articles specifically addressing religious freedom and the rights of ethnic minorities, is adopted.

1994   China's State Ethnic Affairs Commission rules that the government will not recognize any new ethnic groups. According to the government, there are 56 legitimate national minority groups in China.

2002   The United States declares the East Turkestan Islamic Movement an international terrorist organization, a designation that gives greater latitude to the Chinese government to crack down on Uyghur separatism as part of the "war on terrorism."

2005   The PRC continues to crack down on separatists in Xinjiang, although many in the Western media believe that China has inflated the danger of Uyghur separatism.

Allah—the name Muslims use for God; Arabic for "Father."

Cultural Revolution—the period from 1966 to 1976 during which the government attempted to purify China by eliminating "capitalists." Intellectuals and dissenters were oppressed and "re-educated" in state-run camps, while much of China's cultural heritage was destroyed by state-sponsored Red Guards.

dynasty—a group of rulers that maintains power for several generations, with succession typically determined by blood relationship.

ethnic group—a people that has different national or cultural traditions from the majority of the population.

Hadith—a collection of stories about Muhammad and his early Muslim companions; each individual story is also called a hadith.

Hajj—a ritual pilgrimage to Mecca that devout Muslims are required to make at least once during their lifetimes, if they are physically and financially able to do so.

Han—the majority ethnic group within China, making up approximately 92 percent of the population.

Hui—Muslims in China who are descended from early Muslim traders. The Chinese character *Hui* means "those who will return," as these foreign traders expected to one day return to their homes.

Islam—A monotheistic religion established by the Prophet Muhammad in the seventh century. The word *islam* is derived from the Arabic verb *aslama*, which means "to submit"; Muslims believe that by following Muhammad's teachings they are submitting to the will of God.

Muslim—a follower of Islam; one who submits to the will of Allah.

Qu'ran—The sacred scriptures of Islam, believed by Muslims to contain the revelations of God to the Prophet Mohammad. The original text is in Arabic and the devout learn that language in order to read it exactly as the scripture was written.

separatist—one who secedes or advocates separation from an established nation-state.

Glossary

shamanism—using priests or priestesses skilled in magic to communicate with the gods, control events, and cure the sick.

Silk Road—the name for ancient trade routes across Asia that linked China with the eastern Mediterranean and Europe. Although the trade routes originally connected the Roman empire and the Han dynasty about 2,000 years ago, the name "Silk Road" was not coined until the 19th century.

Sufism—a mystical movement within Islam, in which Muslims seek a closer personal relationship with Allah. Sufis believe they can draw closer to God by performing certain spiritual disciplines, such as prayer, ritual chanting, and ecstatic dancing.

Sunni Islam—the larger of the two main branches of Islam. More than 80 percent of the world's Muslims are Sunnis. Most Chinese Muslims are Sunnis.

Uyghur—the name used to denote descendants of various Turkic tribes living in western China (particularly the Xinjiang province).

Bulag, Uradyn E. *The Mongols at China's Edge: History and the Politics of National Unity*. Lanham, Md.: Rowman and Littlefield, 2002.

Dillon, Michael. *China's Muslim Hui Community: Migration, Settlement and Sects*. Richmond, England: Curzon, 1999.

Dreyer, June Teufel. *China's Forty Million: Minority Nationalities and National Integration in the People's Republic of China*. Cambridge, Mass.: Harvard University Press, 1976.

Eberhard, Wolfram. *China's Minorities: Yesterday and Today*. Belmont, Calif.: Wadsworth Publishing, 1982.

Emerick, Yahiya. *Understanding Islam*. Indianapolis: Alpha, 2002.

Esposito, John L., ed. *The Oxford History of Islam*. New York: Oxford University Press, 1999.

Fewsmith, Joseph. *China Since Tiananmen: The Politics of Transition*. New York: Cambridge University Press, 2001.

Gladney, Dru C. *Muslim Chinese: Ethnic Nationalism in the People's Republic*. Cambridge, Mass.: Harvard University Press, 1991.

Harrell, Stevan, ed. *Cultural Encounters on China's Ethnic Frontiers*. Seattle: University of Washington Press, 1994.

Hattstein, Markus. *World Religions*. Cologne, Germany: Koneman, 1999.

Haw, Stephen G. *A Traveller's History of China*. New York: Interlink Books, 1995.

Heberer, Thomas. *China and its National Minorities: Autonomy or Assimilation?* Armonk, N.Y.: M.E. Sharpe, 1989.

Lampton, David M. *Same Bed, Different Dreams: Managing U.S.-China Relations 1989–2000*. Berkeley: University of California Press, 2001.

Lieberthal, Kenneth. *Governing China: From Revolution Through Reform*. 2nd ed. New York: W. W. Norton & Co., 2004.

Further Reading

Ma, Yin. *China's Minority Nationalities*. Beijing: Foreign Language Press, 1989.

Mackerras, Colin. *China's Minorities: Integration and Modernisation in the Twentieth Century*. Hong Kong: Oxford University Press, 1994.

————. *China's Minority Cultures: Identities and Integration Since 1912*. New York: St. Martin's Press, 1995.

Morris, Neil. *The Atlas of Islam: People, Daily Life and Traditions*. Hauppauge, N.J.: Barrons Educational Series, 2003.

Moser, Leo J. *The Chinese Mosaic: The Peoples and Provinces of China*. Boulder, Colo., and London: Westview Press, 1985.

Ruthven, Malise. *Islam in the World*. New York: Oxford University Press, 2000.

Rossabi, Morris, ed. *Governing China's Multiethnic Frontiers*. Seattle: University of Washington Press, 2004.

Rudelson, Justin Jon. *Oasis Identities: Uighur Nationalism Along China's Silk Road*. New York: Columbia University Press, 1997.

Spence, Jonathan D. *The Search for Modern China*. New York: W. W. Norton & Co., 1999.

Stuart-Fox, Martin. *A Short History of China and Southeast Asia: Tribute Trade, and Influence*. London: Allyn & Unwin, 2003.

Swisher, Clarice, ed. *The Spread of Islam*. San Diego: Greenhaven Press, 1998.

Terrill, Ross. *Mao: A Biography*. Stanford, Calif.: Stanford University Press, 1999.

Wang, James C. F. *Contemporary Chinese Politics: An Introduction*. 7th ed. Englewood Cliffs, N.J.: Prentice Hall, 2001.

Yang, Benjamin. *Deng: A Political Biography*. Armonk, N.Y.: M. E. Sharpe, 1998.

http://www.chinadaily.com.cn/english/home/index.html

English language on-line version of *China Daily*, the most popular daily newspaper in China.

http://english.peopledaily.com.cn/

English language on-line version of the official state newspaper, *People's Daily.*

http://www.china.org.cn/english/

English language version of official state information site, includes news, history, white papers, and the text of official policies.

http://www.geocities.com/WestHollywood/Park/6443/China/

Links to various sites on Islam in China.

http://www.ehalal.net/china/overview.html

Overview about Muslims in China. Includes excellent maps.

http://www.chinaculture.org/gb/en/node_2.htm

The official Chinese Culture Ministry's website includes many articles and maps related to ethnic minorities.

http://www.rferl.org/featuresarticle/2004/06/f98dd1f2-f669-4d00-aabf-f9c096b423a1.html

Radio Free Europe/Radio Liberty's activist Muslim issues regarding China and Central Asian nations

http://english.peopledaily.com.cn/constitution/constitution.html

The text, in English, of the constitution of the People's Republic of China.

http://web.umr.edu/~msaumr/Quran/

This site provides a searchable English translation of the Qur'an, organized by chapter.

http://www.cia.gov/cia/publications/factbook/geos/ch.html

The CIA World Factbook provides a wealth of statistical and other information about China and its ethnic groups.

Internet Resources

http://www.redflag.info/minorities.htm

Provides links to hundreds of websites about China's 56 ethnic groups.

http://www.china.org.cn/e-groups/shaoshu/index.htm

A comprehensive site on China's ethnic groups, containing information on historical, political, and economic matters.

http://www.chinaleadershipmonitor.org/

China Leadership Monitor is a web-based journal with articles by eminent scholars in the United States on China's leadership.

http://www.china.org.cn/english/index.htm

Information on political, social, economic, and cultural life in China.

Numbers in **bold italic** refer to captions.

Hadith, 18, *24*, *28*
  See also Islam
Han Chinese (ethnic group), *22*,
  23, 39, 55, 72, 100
    See also ethnic groups
Hongkui, Ma, 77
Hongxi (Emperor), 49
Hui Muslims, 38–39, 47, *52*,
  55–58, 72–77
    See also ethnic groups
Hulegü Khan, 35
human rights, 85–86, 101–102

Indonesia, 45
Islam
  and Abraham, 15–16, 19
  five pillars of, 18–19
  founding and spread of, 17–19,
    25, 27–29, 45
  influence of, on Chinese culture,
    37–51
  number of followers, in China,
    12, 21–23, 55
  protection of, under the constitu-
    tion, 86–89
  reform, 72–73
  Shia, 65
  spread of, to China, 13, 19–21,
    24, 29–35
  Sufism, 59–60, 72–73
  Sunni, 56, 59–60, 65, 68
  See also ethnic groups
Islamism, 90
  See also Islam

Jahriyya Naqshbandi, 73

See also reform movements in
  Islam
Jamae Mosque, 90
Judaism, 15–16, 19

Kabul, 32
Kazakhs (ethnic group), 61, 62–63,
  64
    See also ethnic groups
Khuffiya Naqshbandi, 73
    See also reform movements in
    Islam
Kublai Khan, 34, 35, 45, 47
Kyrgyz (ethnic groups), 61, 63–64
    See also ethnic groups

languages, 56, 67, 68
Liao dynasty, 41
Linxia, 65

Ma He. See Zheng He
Malaysia, 45
Manchu dynasty. See Qing dynasty
"mandate of heaven," 14
    See also world view (traditional
    Chinese)
Mao Zedong, 54, 67, *70*, 76–79,
  84
Mecca, 18, 19, *20*, 27–28, 49, 93
Medina, 18, 25, 27–28
Middle Kingdom, 26–27, 48–49
    See also China
military, 44
Ming dynasty, 42, 47–48
Mingxin, Ma, 73
Mongols, 34–35, 41, 45, 47, 48–49,

Index

Picture Credits

Page

6: Nik Wheeler/Saudi Aramco World/PADIA
8: © OTTN Publishing
12: Nik Wheeler/Saudi Aramco World/PADIA
15: Corbis Images
16: Tor Eigeland/Saudi Aramco World/PADIA
20: S.M. Amin/Saudi Aramco World/PADIA
22: Nik Wheeler/Saudi Aramco World/PADIA
24: China Photos/Getty Images
28: (both images) Dick Doughty/Saudi Aramco World/PADIA
31: Nik Wheeler/Saudi Aramco World/PADIA
33: Nik Wheeler/Saudi Aramco World/PADIA
35: MPI/Getty Images
36: Nik Wheeler/Saudi Aramco World/PADIA
39: Tor Eigeland/Saudi Aramco World/PADIA
41: Nik Wheeler/Saudi Aramco World/PADIA
42: Nik Wheeler/Saudi Aramco World/PADIA
43: Asian Art & Archaeology, Inc./Corbis
46: Bibliotheque Nationale, Paris
50: Nik Wheeler/Saudi Aramco World/PADIA
52: Nik Wheeler/Saudi Aramco World/PADIA
57: Nik Wheeler/Saudi Aramco World/PADIA

58: Nik Wheeler/Saudi Aramco World/PADIA
60: Nik Wheeler/Saudi Aramco World/PADIA
61: Nik Wheeler/Saudi Aramco World/PADIA
63: Tor Eigeland/Saudi Aramco World/PADIA
64: Nik Wheeler/Saudi Aramco World/PADIA
67: Nik Wheeler/Saudi Aramco World/PADIA
70: Tor Eigeland/Saudi Aramco World/PADIA
75: National Archives & Records Administration
76: Library of Congress
78: Library of Congress
80: Hulton Archive/Getty Images
82: National Archives & Records Administration
84: National Archives & Records Administration
86: Corbis Images
88: Tor Eigeland/Saudi Aramco World/PADIA
91: Nik Wheeler/Saudi Aramco World/PADIA
94: Nik Wheeler/Saudi Aramco World/PADIA
96: Nik Wheeler/Saudi Aramco World/PADIA
99: Nik Wheeler/Saudi Aramco World/PADIA
102: Nik Wheeler/Saudi Aramco World/PADIA
104: Frederic J. Brown/AFP/Getty Images

Front cover: IMS Communications, Ltd. (background); Nik Wheeler/Saudi Aramco World/PADIA (inset)
Back cover: Nik Wheeler/Saudi Aramco World/PADIA

The **FOREIGN POLICY RESEARCH INSTITUTE (FPRI)** served as editorial consultants for the GROWTH AND INFLUENCE OF ISLAM IN THE NATIONS OF ASIA AND CENTRAL ASIA series. FPRI is one of the nation's oldest "think tanks." The Institute's Middle East Program focuses on Gulf security, monitors the Arab-Israeli peace process, and sponsors an annual conference for teachers on the Middle East, plus periodic briefings on key developments in the region.

Among the FPRI's trustees is a former Secretary of State and a former Secretary of the Navy (and among the FPRI's former trustees and interns, two current Undersecretaries of Defense), not to mention two university presidents emeritus, a foundation president, and several active or retired corporate CEOs.

The scholars of FPRI include a former aide to three U.S. Secretaries of State, a Pulitzer Prize–winning historian, a former president of Swarthmore College and a Bancroft Prize–winning historian, and two former staff members of the National Security Council. And the FPRI counts among its extended network of scholars—especially its Inter-University Study Groups—representatives of diverse disciplines, including political science, history, economics, law, management, religion, sociology, and psychology.

DR. HARVEY SICHERMAN is president and director of the Foreign Policy Research Institute in Philadelphia, Pennsylvania. He has extensive experience in writing, research, and analysis of U.S. foreign and national security policy, both in government and out. He served as Special Assistant to Secretary of State Alexander M. Haig Jr. and as a member of the Policy Planning Staff of Secretary of State James A. Baker III. Dr. Sicherman was also a consultant to Secretary of the Navy John F. Lehman Jr. (1982–1987) and Secretary of State George Shultz (1988).

A graduate of the University of Scranton (B.S., History, 1966), Dr. Sicherman earned his Ph.D. at the University of Pennsylvania (Political Science, 1971), where he received a Salvatori Fellowship. He is author or editor of numerous books and articles, including *America the Vulnerable: Our Military Problems and How to Fix Them* (FPRI, 2002) and *Palestinian Autonomy, Self-Government and Peace* (Westview Press, 1993). He edits *Peacefacts*, an FPRI bulletin that monitors the Arab-Israeli peace process.

SHEILA HOLLIHAN-ELLIOT has written several books on China's history and culture, including *Chinese Art and Architecture* and *The Ancient History of China*. She has been fascinated with Chinese culture since she was a child and her father did business in the country during the 1950s. She has spent time studying firsthand the history, arts, and enormous social and political changes occurring in China today. She is a graduate of Vassar College, and is a member of The China Institute in New York City.